The Great Indian Academic Adventure

Timir Tripathi

ISBN
Paperback 979-8-89673-441-3
Hardcase 979-8-89724-523-9

Contents

Preface

India has always been known as a land of great thinkers, philosophers, innovators, and pioneers, who made important contributions to various fields like mathematics, medicine, and astronomy that have shaped the world. Its traditional knowledge systems (Bhāratīya Jñāna Paramparā), known for combining different fields of study, still inspire modern academics. However, today's Indian academic world faces challenges in fully unlocking its vast potential, as it works to adapt to evolving needs and modern expectations.

This book takes you on a witty and sarcastic journey through the colorful world of Indian academic life, where moments of brilliance mix with quirky situations to create stories that entertain and make you think. It shares fictional tales that uncover the hidden struggles, ironies, and achievements of faculties and researchers in Indian academia. While humor leads the way, the deeper aim of the book is to highlight the challenges in India's research ecosystem and inspire thoughts on how to address them.

Indian academia is a unique world where professors balance teaching, research, and administration like skilled jugglers; young faculties work in low-budget labs with creativity that feels almost magical; and collaboration, mentorship, and innovation sometimes feel out of reach. Through these stories, we meet vibrant characters—a night owl researcher fueled by coffee and curiosity, a young academic navigating the "publish or perish" pressure, and a team trying to bridge the gap between traditional methods and modern technology. Each tale, though fictional, reflects the real-life experiences of many in Indian universities.

This book doesn't just point out the problems in Indian academia—it also tries to explore ways to address them. Each chapter ends with two sections: *Take Home*, which sums up the main lessons from the story and offers possible solutions, and *The Future of Research in India*, which looks at the bigger picture. These sections discuss ideas on how Indian academia can evolve and better support its researchers and society as a whole.

At the center of this book is the National Education Policy (NEP) 2020, a forward-thinking strategic vision that is aimed at solving many of the challenges highlighted in this book. The NEP 2020 focuses on linking teaching and research, promoting multidisciplinary institutions, better funding for research, and encouraging collaboration. It proposes setting up research-focused universities to boost innovation and global competitiveness. It also emphasizes blending our rich intellectual traditions with modern academic needs. This book engages with NEP 2020, not expecting it to be a complete solution but as an optimistic and positive starting point. Through its narratives, the book shows how the ideas behind the policy could address key issues, like improving mentorship, balancing teaching with research, and valuing creativity over traditional mindsets. The narratives reflect the potential of NEP 2020 to transform Indian academia while also recognizing the hurdles in making it a reality.

Ultimately, this book is not just about the challenges of today but also about the possibilities for tomorrow. Indian universities are at a turning point, with the chance to become centers of innovation, collaboration, and excellence. Achieving this will require all stakeholders—professors, administrators, policymakers, and students—to work together, break free from entrenched habits, and embrace a mindset that values curiosity, critical thinking, and meaningful contributions to make India as a hub for global knowledge.

As you dive into these tales of chaos and creativity, my hope is that you will laugh, reflect, and perhaps feel inspired. The journey to a brighter future for Indian academia is long and winding, but it is a journey worth undertaking. Let's imagine a system where teaching and research go hand in hand, young minds are nurtured with care, and the pursuit of knowledge is driven by curiosity and passion.

Welcome to the world of Indian academic life—perfectly imperfect, seriously funny, and, above all, chaotically well-organized.

Timir Tripathi

The Great Indian Juggling Act of Teaching, Research, and Administration

In the grand drama of Indian academia, professors are like jugglers. But here is the twist: there is no grand stage, no cheering crowd, and definitely no applause to make it all seem worthwhile. It is like they are performing on a stage where the audience forgot to show up, doing an act that only they understand. Picture this: a professor trying to juggle three flaming torches called "teaching," "administration," and "research" while balancing on a tightrope of tight deadlines and endless stress. It is not just impressive; it is nearly impossible (like a superhero feat, but without any praise or glory). One hand is busy flipping through a student's thesis—each paragraph an adventure in strange grammar and doubtful facts. On the other hand, there is a pile of paperwork that should have been filed yesterday for an upcoming conference, which promises even more work in the name of academic growth. Meanwhile, in the background, a research seminar is going on. Our tired professor somehow nods wisely, pretending to be very interested, while he is mentally adding "review seminar notes" to a to-do list that is already longer than a PhD thesis.

But how do professors manage this chaotic performance? Is it some kind of secret trick? Do they have extra hours hidden away, like a magician with a hidden deck of cards? Or is the truth that they don't manage it as well as it seems? Maybe the real magic is that they keep going at all through caffeine, hope, and the rare spark of inspiration. Let us take a closer look at this, with a dose of sarcasm, lots of knowing nods, and just enough laughter to stop us from crying.

Chapter 1: The "Professor's Three-Headed Role"

Imagine this: you are an expert in your research field—let's say protein biochemistry, just for fun. You have spent years studying complex molecules and doing experiments that would make anyone's head spin. Suddenly, one day, you hear the words, "Congratulations, Professor! You are now in charge of organizing the annual university cultural festival." Yes, you heard it right. One moment you are focused on lab work and academic papers, and the next, you are choosing performers and planning the food menu. In Indian universities, multitasking is as common as tea stalls on every street. If you are a professor, you are not just one thing; you are a teacher, an administrator, a researcher, and sometimes even an event planner—all in one.

Teaching is the 'Main Job' that comes with surprises

Teaching is the part of the job that most people see as noble and rewarding. It is thought to be the main reason for being a professor. But let's be honest—it often feels like a race against time. Every class is a challenge: "How much of the syllabus can I cover before exams start?" You stand in front of a classroom, sharing your knowledge while handling students, some of whom think that asking, "Will this be on the exam?" is a smart question. Then, there is the huge pile of exam answer scripts waiting to be graded. Each script is a test of your patience, especially when you read answers that make you wonder if you actually know anything. And the handwriting? It's like an ant dipped in ink, trying to find its way around (except the ant itself probably doesn't know where it's going either!) By the end of a long day of teaching and grading, you can't help but wonder—did I choose this job, or did it choose me as part of some cosmic prank?

Administration is the 'Surprise Job' no one tells you about

Now, let us talk about administration, the surprise part of being a professor. This role is like a younger sibling who always wants to join in, whether you want them to or not. You might start your day planning to focus on your research or lectures, but the administration has other ideas. Every professor in an Indian university knows that look—the one that says, "I'm lost in paperwork and I can't escape." There are endless meetings that lead to even more meetings, planning university events that somehow always pop up at the last minute, and programs that test your patience. And, of course, budget cuts! They are the extra challenge that turns simple tasks into hard puzzles. Handling all this feels as fun as cleaning up after a bunch of messy pigeons—frustrating, never-ending, and something you just can't avoid!

Research is the part that is meant to be 'Exciting'

Research is supposed to be the exciting part of being a professor—the part that makes all the hard work worth it. This is where professors dream of making new discoveries and contributing something valuable to their field. But, research often gets stuck under paperwork and long delays. Want to apply for a grant? Be ready for a process that moves as slowly as traffic in Bengaluru during rush hour. And if you manage to finish your research, publishing it is another struggle. You send your paper and then wait forever for overworked reviewers (who are also professors) to respond, who are also busy with their own teaching and administration. By the time you get the review comments months later, you might have even forgotten what your paper was about.

Chapter 2: The "Balancing Act"

The 'Choose Two' rule

In a perfect world (which, let's be honest, doesn't exist in Indian universities), professors would handle teaching, administration, and research like pros, without a single worry. They would switch between giving lectures, running experiments, and filling out reports as if it were second nature. But in the real world, professors soon learn that they can maximally pick two of these roles to focus on. Yes, that's right—just two. It is like playing a really tiring version of "Choose Your Own Adventure," but none of the endings are happy.

If you decide to focus on teaching and research, congrats! You will now be in charge of multiple administrative works that come with zero training or heads-up. Expect to get emails with all-caps subject lines like "URGENT—SUBMIT REPORT BY YESTERDAY." Of course, there is no way you could have known about these reports ahead of time because, for some reason, administrative tasks only appear at the last minute.

If you choose to focus on teaching and administration, say goodbye to your research dreams. Writing papers and applying for grants? Forget it. Your research ideas will sit around in drafts for so long that they will start to wonder what they were even about.

Now, if you decide to take on the bold challenge of balancing research and administration (two things that will drain your energy), get ready for chaos. If you somehow manage to juggle both, your students will probably start calling your lectures "experimental." You won't be making groundbreaking discoveries; instead, you will be perfecting the art of improvising it in front of your class while handling a mountain of admin work. You will leave the classroom thinking, "Well, that was... something," while your students are just glad they made it through without needing a rescue team.

Chapter 3: The "Heroic Story of Dr. Banerjee"

Let's talk about Dr. Banerjee (real in spirit, fictional in detail). Dr. Banerjee is a famous biologist with an impressive academic record. But one fateful evening, he found himself doing something no biologist ever trains for: arranging chairs for a symposium. How did he end up here, you ask? The event coordinator mysteriously vanished, leaving Dr. Banerjee, already running on fumes, to step in. And, being the overachiever he is, he didn't stop there. The next morning, he was back at it, delivering a lecture to a classroom full of confused students who were not sure if they were attending a class or witnessing a bizarre one-person show. Afterward, he spent hours grading 100 exam scripts, each filled with answers more creative than the last. Just when he thought the day was over, he opened his email to find a memo titled: "Mandatory Meeting on Effective Time Management." Oh, the irony.

Dr. Banerjee's story is not unique—it is the perfect example of life in Indian academia, where professors juggle teaching, administration, and research like a never-ending circus act. It is chaos wrapped in more chaos, tied up with red tape. But hey, at least Dr. Banerjee has plenty of material for storytelling (if he ever finds time to leave campus).

Chapter 4: The "Special Chaos"

Meetings are the 'Time-Swallowing Black Hole'

If there is one thing Indians absolutely love, it is meetings. And let me tell you, meetings in Indian universities are not just gatherings. They are an experience. But mostly, not the fun kind. These meetings are a unique kind of torture that only the brave (or unlucky) souls who attend them can truly understand.

You know the drill. The meeting starts with a grand list of agenda and promises to solve all problems of the university. Four hours later, you are still discussing point number one and wondering if this is some elaborate experiment to test your willpower. The best part? In the end, in many cases, the only decision made is to schedule another meeting. Progress? What's that?

And let's not forget the latecomers. Every single time, someone walks in, looks around innocently, and asks, "So, what did I miss?" And the answer (without fail) is mostly the same: "Nothing. Almost nothing. We are still debating the same thing we started with hours ago."

These meetings can be about absolutely anything—planning the annual cultural fest, deciding next year's budget (spoiler alert: it's always too little), or the critically important issue of what samosas the canteen should serve (because clearly, that will save the university). The real question is: why do we keep attending them? The answer? This is an unwritten rule in academia: you must sit through endless discussions and act like something meaningful is happening.

Of course, no meeting is complete without that one professor who loves to go off-topic. While the rest of us stare at the clock, he spends 30 minutes passionately discussing something completely irrelevant—like the history of samosas instead of the canteen menu. Meanwhile, the rest of us sit there, staring at the clock, praying for lunch packets to arrive and rescue us from this agony.

By the time the meeting finally ends, you have lost an entire afternoon and gained nothing of real substance. You leave the room not just drained but slightly less intelligent than when you walked in. Such meetings don't just drain your time; they take a piece of your soul with them. But hey, at least you will walk out with a vague action item to pretend you will follow up on.

Funding is the 'Mirage in the Desert'

Ah, funding—the unicorn of the academic world. Every professor dreams of securing a big research grant that will cover their groundbreaking work, buy shiny equipment, and maybe, just maybe, give them a chance to sleep like a normal human. But here is the catch: funding is like a mirage in the desert. It looks so real from a distance, but the closer you get, the faster it disappears.

Everyone talks about it like it is common: "Oh, just apply for that grant!" they say. But when you actually apply, you realize it is as mythical as a unicorn riding a rainbow. Sure, you might know someone in the university who once heard of someone else getting it, but actually seeing it for yourself? Keep dreaming. It is the ultimate academic tease, always out of reach and always leaving you thirstier than before.

Applying for grants is like running a marathon with no finish line. First, you fill out endless forms, gather references, and write a proposal so long it feels like you have written a novel. Then, after submitting, there comes the waiting. Oh, the waiting. Months turn into a year, and just when you have given up hope, you get the email: your project grant is approved! "Is this real?" you think, pinching yourself in disbelief.

But hold on—this is academia, so the fun doesn't end there. Next comes a parade of paperwork: declarations, mandate forms, undertakings, clearance certificates, equipment non-availability certificates, conflict of interest statements, and who knows what else the funding agency might require. The funds? They will stay out of reach until every single document is submitted. And, of course, preparing and collecting all these forms means multiple trips to the administration—interrupting your classes, research, and countless other responsibilities along the way.

By the time the money finally arrives (after what feels like a geological age), your research idea might have become outdated, or the equipment you wanted is now as obsolete as floppy disks. It is like ordering a fancy gadget online, forgetting about it, and then receiving it years later when no one even remembers what it is for.

The money shows up, but your excitement? Gone. Your project? Dusty.

Welcome to academic life, an endless loop of waiting, hoping, and thinking, "Maybe next time will be better." And don't worry; there is always another grant proposal to prepare and another meeting to discuss it.

Chapter 5: The "Coping Mechanisms"

Finding your 'Inner Yogi'

Surviving in Indian universities is like living in a wild jungle, where professors master the ancient art of "yogic detachment" just to make it through the day. It is that calm, zen-like state that helps you smile when the registrar emails you again, asking for a "comprehensive report" on the academic year's achievements—and, surprise, it is due tomorrow morning. Oh, no big deal. You take a deep breath, reach for your chai, and sip it like it is the ultimate cure for all problems. "Everything's fine," you tell yourself, ignoring the chaos swirling around your mind. The secret survival mantra? "Just one more day." Somehow, that little phrase keeps you going, even when it feels like the whole system is held together by duct tape and sheer willpower.

You know you have truly reached full yogic mode when you see an email with "URGENT" in the subject line, and your first thought is, "Well, there goes my weekend." But instead of panicking, you calmly take another sip of chai and think, "This is what I signed up for… right?" Or maybe you didn't, but by now, you have become an expert at pretending everything is fine while juggling more tasks than a circus master.

Inner peace? Not exactly. It is more like, "inner, please let me survive this day." But somehow, it works. You power through, chai in hand, and convince yourself that you are totally in control, even if you are not.

The myth of 'Work-Life Balance'

Oh yes, the idea of work-life balance, the mythical creature every professor in India is told to chase, as if it is just waiting around the corner. If you have ever heard someone talk about "work-life balance," you probably had the same thought as everyone else: What does that even mean? The reality? Work-life balance is as real as a dragon—everyone talks about it, but no one has ever actually seen it.

In reality, professors don't balance work and life; they juggle endless paperwork, student issues, last-minute meetings, and the occasional existential crisis, all while trying to look like they have a life outside work. Instead of balancing work and life, they rely on caffeine, sarcasm, and late-night "why-did-I-choose-this-career" moments to survive.

A good day is when you don't immediately regret your life choices. A great day? That's when you finally get home, jump on the couch, and stare blankly at the wall, just trying to process it all.

And then comes the classic line: "It will get better once the semester ends." But wait, what's that? Oh, right, the next semester starts the very next day.

Sweet, sweet balance—always a dream, never a reality.

The 'Support System'

Now, let's take a moment to appreciate the true heroes of academia: research students. These champions don't just help with experiments—they save professors from losing their sanity. Without them, many professors would either spontaneously combust from stress or seriously consider quitting to pursue a career with less paperwork—like lion taming or rocket science.

Sure, they do research, but they also take on the unspoken and unexpected responsibilities of academic life. Need someone to proofread your slides at 11 PM? They are on it. Forgot to set up the laptop for a conference? Don't worry; they have already fixed it. These multitasking legends keep the academic machine running, one thankless task at a time.

And let's not forget the lifesavers—the friends from other universities and institutes who understand your pain and fight the same battles. They are the ones who send you memes about academic life that hit so close to your heart that you have to laugh to keep from crying. They know the exact meme to send when it's Friday afternoon, and you are staring at your to-do list, wondering if it is secretly multiplying.

In Indian universities, without a strong support system, whether it's your trusty research students, those meme-sending friends, or just someone to say, "Hang in there; we are all doomed together," it is difficult to survive. Because let's face it, sometimes, it's humor, teamwork, and the occasional WhatsApp group chat that keep the whole thing from collapsing.

Take Home—Can it be fixed?

Dreaming big, starting small

So, can we fix the chaos of Indian academia? Maybe not all at once, but with some thoughtful changes and a shift in attitude, it is definitely possible. The first step is understanding that professors are human, not machines. Once we realize that, we can start building an academic environment where professors don't just survive but thrive.

For starters, universities need more administrative staff to handle the endless paperwork. Right now, professors are expected to do everything, and that includes tasks that have nothing to do with teaching or research. If someone else managed the paperwork, professors could actually focus on what they are supposed to do—teach, research, and inspire students. Imagine that!

Another thing that could help is making grant applications simpler. Right now, the process for applying for funding feels like playing a video game where the rules make no sense, and the boss level is a 50-page form asking for details you can't even guess. Simplifying the process would be a huge relief. If getting research funding didn't feel like solving a puzzle from a spy movie, professors could actually spend their time on, well, research.

Technology as a friend or a foe

Let us talk about technology. It can either be a professor's best friend or their worst enemy, depending on whether it is having a good day or not. When it works, it is amazing. Imagine a university portal that actually does what it is supposed to do—uploading grades, managing records, and not freezing when you need it most. It is like stepping into a world where everything just clicks. But, oh, when it doesn't work? That is when the trouble begins. Picture this: you are rushing to upload exam marks before a lecture, and boom, the system crashes. Suddenly, your calm day turns into a stressful mess, with emails flying everywhere and a few choice words muttered under your breath.

But here is the thing: if technology is used wisely, it could make life so much easier. Think about automating repetitive tasks, simplifying record management, and making virtual meetings a breeze. Professors could finally stop chasing paper forms, sending a hundred emails to organize one event, and dealing with tech glitches that threaten to ruin their day. It would be like walking out of the dark ages and into a world where professors are no longer stuck doing everything the hard way. Technology could be a real game-changer, if only it would cooperate seamlessly.

Creating a culture of support

Here is an idea that might sound a little radical: creating a supportive, not competitive, environment among professors. It might seem strange, but hear me out. When professors work together as a team instead of constantly competing, amazing things can happen. Cooperation (even a little bit) can make a huge difference in research productivity and the overall mood on campus.

Mentorship programs could really help, too. New professors often feel completely lost, not knowing how to handle all the work. Having a senior professor guide them through the maze of work and expectations could relieve a lot of that stress. It is also important for universities to recognize just how hard balancing everything is. When universities show that they get it, it sends a strong message: "We understand. It is tough. And we are here to help." Even simple gestures, like regular check-ins or open conversations about workloads, can make new professors feel supported and less isolated.

These changes would not magically fix everything, but they are a good start. Professors are not asking for the moon—just a system that works without breaking them in the process. Let's make it happen.

The Future of Research in India— The Balancing Act Continues

Trying to balance teaching, administration, and research in Indian universities is more like an art than a science—chaotic, messy, and often frustrating. It is the kind of art where you look at it and wonder, "Is this genius, or did the artist just throw paint at the canvas and call it a day?" Professors in India have turned this juggling act into a survival skill because, let's face it, there is no other option. The show must go on, even if it is a show no one asked for.

In the middle of all these deadlines, meetings, and last-minute tasks, Indian professors have developed a special kind of resilience. They have mastered the art of hearing "manage your time better" and responding with a smile that says, "Thanks for the tip." It is the ability to turn a day planned for teaching and research into an emergency meeting about the university's new mascot. It is the determination to say, "Yes, I can handle one more thing," even when their schedule is packed tighter than a Mumbai local train during rush hour.

And yet, they keep going. Why? Because in Indian academia, stopping is not an option. No matter how wild things get, the work must continue. With a smile that says, "I cannot believe this is happening," a sigh that shows all the tasks still waiting to be done, and a cup of chai in hand, they somehow make it through another day. It is not perfect, and it is rarely pretty, but it's theirs. This is what keeps Indian universities running—a mix of determination, humor, and just enough caffeine to power through.

So, while balancing everything might never get easier, Indian professors have shown they can handle it, even if it feels like juggling flaming swords. And in true Indian style, the day ends not with praise or applause but with a shared laugh and the promise of more madness tomorrow. But don't worry—they will be ready, chai in hand, for whatever comes next.

So, how is NEP 2020 helping with this juggling act? NEP 2020 sees the chaos and aims to fix it. It promotes interdisciplinary research, encourages collaboration between departments and institutions, and works to cut down the paperwork that slows things down. With clearer policies, better research funding, and less red tape, NEP 2020 is setting the stage for a smoother, more supportive academic world. This could mean professors spend less time managing tasks and more time focusing on what they do best— innovating and mentoring.

Disclaimer: *This chapter might exaggerate for effect (or not), but the truth is clear: teaching, administration, and research each deserve full attention. Whether that balance will be found soon or not, one thing is certain: no professor will ever say no to a little extra help, a quicker process, and a slightly lighter load. Until then, the juggling continues.*

The Dream Team of Teaching and Research

In the busy world of higher education in India, it often feels like everyone is racing in circles, desperately trying to find their way. Professors are buried under mountains of assignments, lectures, and paperwork, while students are often confused, wondering if they are in the right class. Amid all this chaos, one crucial connection is often ignored that ties everything together: the glaring elephant in the room—the link between teaching and research. Professors usually get caught up in the routine of lectures and grading, but this focus can sometimes push research to the side. The NEP 2020 has highlighted the need for teaching and research to work hand in hand, showing how research can make teaching better and create a more engaging learning environment. Research not only helps students develop critical thinking and creativity but also keeps academic fields alive and growing. Both teachers and students need to understand the value of research in education.

So, as we navigate the complex world of higher education, it is essential for both professors and researchers to recognize the power of research. Let us take a light-hearted look at the colorful characters in this bustling world of higher education and the one important thing they seem to overlook: the need to embrace research alongside their noble teaching efforts.

Chapter 1: The "Teaching Titans"

Meet our Teaching Titans—the professors who stride confidently into lecture halls with chalk in hand like swords and an air of authority that could rival any superhero (if superheroes were a bit outdated). They are the guardians of knowledge, shaping young minds with wisdom (or at least with a syllabus that was cutting-edge five years ago). But here is the twist: while their passion for teaching is undeniable, their research contributions are as noticeable as a light breeze—barely there.

Picture this: Prof. Singh is a master of the lecture hall and laser-focused on delivering an electrifying lecture on the fundamental concepts of his field. The clock ticks down as he masterfully spins tales of theoretical frameworks while students nod along (well, at least the ones who haven't drifted off to dreamland). Meanwhile, over in the corner, there is a poster of NEP 2020 urging for "a vibrant research ecosystem" as if it is whispering to him, "Hey, Professor, research could be the dessert that completes the meal. You would not just skip it altogether, would you?"

In the current academic scenario in India, it is high time our Teaching Titans understand that teaching and research can actually go hand in hand. They need to embrace research with the same enthusiasm they have for their teaching—because, believe it or not, a sprinkle of innovation could really spice up their lectures!

So, let us remind these professors that research is not an extra burden; it is the secret ingredient that can transform good teaching into great teaching. Why not step beyond the classroom and bring new ideas to life? After all, isn't it more rewarding to prepare students for the future rather than the past?

Chapter 2: The "Research Rebels"

Next up, we have the Research Rebels, those brave souls who dive into a world filled with experiments, data analysis, and countless nights spent staring at their glowing computer screens. These passionate researchers are convinced that their groundbreaking work will change the world (or at least a tiny corner of it) if only they could remember to actually hit the "submit" button on those long-overdue papers. Their offices? Oh, they look like scenes straight out of horror movies, filled with coffee cups that have become a part of science experiments themselves.

Take Dr. Mukherjee, for example. She is a true Research Rebel. Her academic achievements are as impressive as a magician pulling rabbits out of hats. She thrives in the chaos of her lab, where beakers bubble and data points dance. But whenever she tries to make time for teaching, it is like trying to fit a square peg into a round hole. The result? A comedy of errors, with students wondering, "Isn't she supposed to have a PhD in research, not confusion?"

Dr. Mukherjee's lectures often feel like her experiments—messy and unpredictable. She dives into cutting-edge theories, only to realize midway that her students have mentally checked out into their own TikTok worlds. While she passionately unravels concepts she barely understands herself, the students are left bewildered. Their puzzled expressions could easily inspire the next horror film: "The Curse of the Confounded Class."

Despite her best efforts, Dr. Mukherjee struggles to balance research and teaching. Standing before her class, she often sighs, "Why presenting data is not as easy as collecting it?" Her students, caught in the crossfire of her academic ambitions, leave the classroom more confused than when they entered.

Research Rebels like Dr. Mukherjee are vital to academia, but they need to learn how to mix their chaotic genius with a bit of teaching finesse. Only then can they avoid becoming the subject of an ongoing academic joke and truly inspire the next generation.

Chapter 3: The "Bureaucratic Beast"

Ah, the Bureaucratic Beast—the ultimate killjoy of academia. This creature lurks in the shadows, ready to ambush any research project or collaboration that dares to take shape. With layers of approvals, endless forms, and signature chases, it is enough to make even the most passionate academic want to stick to teaching basic academics.

Meet Dr. Rao, a well-meaning professor with dreams of groundbreaking research. He decides to start a collaboration with another university, thinking it will be an exciting academic adventure. But instead, he finds himself trapped in a bureaucratic swamp. He finds that his email has been forwarded to ten different ten inboxes, each one monitored by officials who are about as helpful as a screen door on a submarine. By the time he finally got the green light, his once-innovative project had gone stale, like fine wine turned to vinegar.

The NEP 2020 talks about a more efficient academic framework, but Dr. Rao's experience feels like a slow-motion disaster. He sits at his desk, sighing, "If only the higher-ups could simplify this process, maybe my research would not die in red tape." Instead of feeling like an innovator, Dr. Rao is stuck in bureaucratic quicksand. His excitement fades as he faces a maze of policies that seem designed to crush his spirit for research.

Ironically, Dr. Rao is not chasing fame, but he is just trying to do something meaningful, something that could actually benefit students and enrich the academic community. Instead, he feels like he is playing a never-ending game of academic ping-pong, where every time he tries to make progress, he just gets slammed back to square one.

In this chaos of inefficiency, it is painfully clear that the real hurdle in academia is not a lack of ideas or passion—it is the bureaucratic beast that thrives on chaos. And so, Dr. Rao waits, hoping for a miracle to pull him out of this endless nightmare and let his research finally see the light of day.

Chapter 4: The "Interdepartmental Olympics"

In this academic world, we also have the Interdepartmental Olympics, where different academic departments compete for resources and recognition. You can practically hear the cheers and boos as the Life Science department goes head-to-head against the Material Science department in a dramatic funding battle royale while English and History engage in their legendary feud. They are so busy trying to prove who is the best that they completely ignore the possibility of working together on some groundbreaking research about historical literature. Instead, they are locked in an endless argument over whether Shakespeare understood human nature better than anyone else (or he just got lucky!)

Meanwhile, students sit in the middle of this tug-of-war, quietly thinking, "Can we just get back to actual work, please?" You can picture it: faculty meetings where the air is thick with tension, as professors hurl their best arguments like dodgeballs. The English professors insist that analyzing Shakespeare's character development is the pinnacle of human thought, while the History professors roll their eyes, claiming that context is everything. It is like watching two stubborn kids argue over who gets the biggest slice of the pie, completely missing the point that they could just share the whole pie.

Students who are trying to figure out their research projects are left scratching their heads, wondering why their professors are not able to see the potential of

Teaching
Research

working together. Instead of pooling their strengths, the departments engage in a war of words that benefits no one. In this absurd competition, the real winner is the bureaucracy, happily sitting back and enjoying the show.

And so, the absurd competition continues while students just want to shout, "Can we focus on real research instead of this endless debate?" But hey, in academia, why work together when you can have a never-ending feud?

Chapter 5: The "Awakening"

And now, dear readers, we arrive at the awakening moment in our tale. With NEP 2020, change is finally sweeping through Indian academia, bringing the revolutionary idea that research isn't just a nice extra—it is crucial for universities to thrive and stay relevant in today's ever-evolving world.

Enter the charming Vice Chancellor, who declares with a smile, "Teaching is great, but have you ever tried doing research? It is like adding chilli to your daal—just a pinch can make everything better!" Some faculty members exchange looks that mix amusement with total confusion. Is this really happening? Could it be the wake-up call they have been waiting for?

Thanks to the NEP 2020, Indian universities are slowly realizing that teaching and research are two sides of the same coin. Faculty members tentatively attend interdisciplinary discussions and journal clubs—at first, with a healthy dose of skepticism, but eventually, to everyone's surprise, with genuine enthusiasm. It is a bit like a comedy show where the characters reluctantly come together, only to find out they make a pretty good team after all.

As these professors dip their toes into the world of research, they discover that it is not as scary as they thought. They might even find that asking questions and exploring new ideas not only enriches their own knowledge but also makes their teaching more exciting. Imagine that! Students who once stared blankly at their notes start asking thoughtful questions that go beyond the textbook. Who would have thought research could breathe new life into the classroom?

The collaborative spirit begins to spread, and departments that once viewed each other as rivals start realizing that they can work together. English and History find themselves in a room discussing the fascinating links between Shakespeare and historical events. Meanwhile, students watch in disbelief, thinking, "Wait, are they actually working together? This is wild!"

But let's not get ahead of ourselves. Not everyone is convinced that this research revolution is a good idea. Some faculty members stubbornly cling to the old ways, insisting that teaching should remain the only focus. They are like the grumpy old uncle (phupha) at a wedding, grumbling about how things were better in the good old days. However, as the new wave of enthusiasm grows, it is becoming harder for them to ignore the benefits of integrating research into their teaching.

As the story unfolds, the academic landscape starts to shift. The once-quiet hallways buzz with excitement as professors work together on research projects, brainstorm ideas, and actually enjoy the process. It is like watching a garden bloom after a long winter—vibrant, hopeful, and full of life.

So, dear readers, the winds of change are here, and they are sweeping through Indian universities like a refreshing breeze. With a bit of support from the higher authorities and the push of the NEP 2020, the once-divided worlds of teaching and research are finally starting to come together. It is a journey filled with laughter, learning, and maybe a few bumps along the way, but isn't that exactly what makes academia such an exciting place to be?

Take Home-Time for integration

As academia evolves, professors learn to juggle their responsibilities. They carve out time for research. "Who knew that research could be as exciting as grading papers?" exclaims Dr. Singh, who has finally figured out that teaching and research can coexist. Who would have thought?

Students are loving this new energy too. Seeing their professors dive into the thrilling world of research, share groundbreaking discoveries in lectures, and weave research outcomes into teaching like little sparks of inspiration adds a whole new spark to the classroom. It's like watching a cake get baked and then getting to taste the result— exciting and satisfying!

As faculty members dive into research, they begin to experience the thrill of innovation. It is like they have discovered a whole new planet beyond their usual classroom orbits. The satisfaction of contributing to the academic world outside the classroom becomes almost addictive.

The once-ignored poster of NEP 2020, which previously collected dust in the corner, now shines like a beacon of hope, guiding them toward a brighter, more balanced academic future.

But let's not pretend like it is all smooth sailing. Balancing teaching and research can be challenging. There are moments when Dr. Singh wonders if he has taken on too much. "Is it too late to start a YouTube channel?" he jokingly asks his colleagues during a coffee break. Yet, every time he doubts himself, he remembers the excitement he felt when he stepped into the research arena. It is exhilarating! Who knew tackling complex problems could be as engaging as reciting the same lecture for the hundredth batch of students?

As professors adapt to this new reality, they are not just transforming their own practices; they are also setting a new standard for students. No longer are they just passive recipients of knowledge; they are now active participants in the research journey. This dynamic shift is helping to create a vibrant academic community where teaching and research are intertwined.

So here is to the professors who are boldly integrating teaching and research, setting new benchmarks, and inspiring their students along the way. It's a wild ride, but it is one worth taking—especially with students cheering them on (without popcorn in hand!)

The Future of Research in India—Bridging Research and Teaching for Innovation and Discovery

So here we are at the grand finale of our academic saga. The Teaching Titans, Research Rebels, and Bureaucratic Beasts have finally found a way to coexist—like a group of mismatched roommates in a sitcom. They now recognize that collaboration and innovation lead to a more vibrant academic ecosystem. As they take their final bows, the audience (consisting of eager students) applauds, ready to embark on their own adventures in this newly revitalized world of higher education.

The lesson is crystal clear: integrating research with teaching is not just a trend; it is essential for the survival of Indian universities in this evolving global landscape. Imagine trying to keep a plant alive without water; that is what universities would be like without research. And while the road may be bumpy, complete with potholes of confusion and speed bumps of bureaucracy, the end goal is worth it: a richer, more impactful academic experience for all.

So, dear reader, the next time you step into a lecture hall, remember the magic of balance. Embrace the chaos and let the spirit of research fuel your teaching journey. After all, in this wild ride of academia, a little chaos can lead to some pretty amazing discoveries. Just think about it: instead of sticking to the dusty old syllabus like a broken record, professors can spice things up with fresh research findings that keep everyone awake and engaged. Who doesn't love a surprise plot twist?

As our academic heroes ride off into the sunset, let us give them a round of applause. Seriously, they deserve it for managing to juggle all their roles—probably with a bit of charm and a whole lot of clumsiness. After all, if there is one thing we can take away from this story, it is that academia is way better when everyone plays nice and works together. Who knew exploring new avenues and teamwork could be so effective? So here is to a future where education is bright and balanced. So, raise your imaginary glasses to the next generation of scholars! May they stumble, fumble, and occasionally laugh their way through their studies. Because in this wild world of academia, a good chuckle can make even the most tedious lecture a little more bearable. Cheers to the unpredictable journey of learning!

Disclaimer: *This story is a light-hearted and fictional take on the world of academia, meant to entertain and maybe tease a little. Any similarity to real professors, students, or administrators is purely accidental (or maybe not), but let's just pretend it is. No Teaching Titans were hurt (except their egos), Research Rebels are still chasing their deadlines, and the Bureaucratic Beast is alive and well. If this hits a little too close to home, don't worry; we are all in the same boat, laughing (or crying) together. Cheers to progress!*

When Two Labs Are Better Than One: Collaboration in Indian Academia

India, a land with a rich intellectual heritage, has been the birthplace of pioneers in mathematics, medicine, and scientific exploration. From the ancient texts of Vedic mathematics to the groundbreaking contributions of thinkers like Sushruta and Aryabhata, our country has historically been a hub of knowledge. Fast forward to the 21st century, and the Indian academic landscape is filled with immense potential, brimming with bright minds and research opportunities. Yet, there is a new realm in modern academia that we have to embrace more fully: collaboration. In today's interconnected world, collaboration has become one of the most powerful drivers of research and innovation. While the image of the lone genius working in isolation still exists, the greatest breakthroughs now occur when researchers unite across disciplines, institutions, and even borders. For Indian universities, the challenge is not a shortage of talent or resources—it is the creation of an ecosystem that encourages teamwork and collective exploration. The good news? This transformation is already within our reach, provided we adopt the open mindset and the right strategies.

So, dear reader, let us embark on a journey into the world of collaboration (or rather, its absence) in Indian universities. If you are imagining an enthusiastic narrator in a lab coat, dramatically waving test tubes while explaining the importance of collaboration, you are not far from the truth. But worry not! We will take a light-hearted yet scientifically sharp look into the critical analysis of why collaboration is the missing ingredient in the research and innovation landscape of India's academic halls. So, grab your pipette (or just your coffee), and let's dive in!

Chapter 1: The "Lone Genius"

You must have heard of the "lone genius" trope, right? The brilliant mind, toiling away in a dimly lit lab, making a groundbreaking discovery that changes the world (a classic "Eureka!" moment). Now, let me ask you a slightly inconvenient question: How realistic is that in the 21st century? Sure, Newton figured out gravity when an apple fell on his head, but the modern-day equivalent involves collaborations across physics, biology, chemistry, and, at times, even a WhatsApp group discussion.

While our universities are brimming with intellectual potential, the "lone genius" narrative often serves as a convenient excuse for the lack of collaboration.

Here is the kicker: while our imaginary, lab-coated researcher with glasses is trying to crack the mysteries of quantum mechanics, his colleague next door (working on organic chemistry) might already have half the solution. The problem? Neither of them knows it because—surprise, surprise—they are not talking. They might as well be working on separate planets, one stuck in a black hole of isolation, the other lost in a solution of disconnected compounds.

This lack of collaboration has become the Achilles' heel of Indian research. There is talent, there is potential, but there is also a severe case of academic myopia. And while everyone is busy doing their own work, innovation continues to suffer from the lack of combined brainpower.

Chapter 2: The "Cross-Pollination"

Collaboration, in a perfect scientific utopia, works much like cross-pollination. Think of it in this way: bees buzzing from flower to flower, transferring pollen and ensuring that life continues to flourish. Now, replace the bees with researchers and the flowers with academic disciplines, and what you have is an image of how collaboration works in theory. The cross-pollination of ideas (researchers from different disciplines collaborating) results in richer, more robust research outcomes.

But, and it's a big "but," Indian universities seem to have adopted a more pollen-allergic approach to academic cross-pollination. In most universities, the Department of "A" is on its own isolated island, rarely, if ever, talking to the Department of "B." These academic silos are so entrenched that getting two different departments to work together is almost as difficult as convincing a physicist to join a poetry club. (Though I would not underestimate physicists, they have got quantum limericks down to an art).

In the real world, interdisciplinary collaboration is where the magic happens. All groundbreaking fields are products of collaborations across disciplines. In India, unfortunately, researchers often remain confined within the four walls of their own discipline, leaving little room for the cross-pollination of ideas. And it is not just limited to universities. Many researchers at institutions also love their silos. Take the IITs, for instance. While they are brilliant at engineering, when was the last time you heard of them teaming up with a university to crack a big pressing problem? Exactly. Such collaborations probably exist, but they are rarer than a solar eclipse on a rainy day. It is like having Batman and Iron Man in the same universe but never teaming up because they each prefer their own unique crime-fighting methods.

Chapter 3: The "Administrative Inertia"

Now, let us dive into the administrative quagmire of Indian academia. If collaboration is the reaction that leads to innovation, lengthy administrative procedures are the inhibitor compound that slows everything down, turning the process into something akin to watching paint dry—underwater. Any researcher who has tried to get a collaborative project approved knows the feeling. First, there is the endless paperwork. Then come the meetings that could have been emails. Finally, by the time all the permissions and signatures have been obtained, the research proposal has often gone stale.

To make things even more delightful, consider the highly decentralized nature of the decision-making processes. Want to collaborate with an international university? Get ready to navigate through a maze of approval channels that would leave even Byomkesh Bakshi scratching his head. From involving the Ministry to securing approval from the UGC, it feels like you need to solve an academic escape room before you can even start collaborating. Meanwhile, other countries, particularly those pesky rivals like China, are speeding ahead with international collaborations, free from such long administrative shackles. Researchers from Chinese universities are racking up collaborative research papers with institutions from the U.S., Europe, and beyond, while we are still stuck waiting for that collaborative MoU to pass through its tenth round of approvals.

Chapter 4: The "Industry-Academia Collaborations"

Ah, industry-academia collaboration—the Bigfoot of Indian research. Everyone talks about it, but rarely people have seen it. In the context of our country, this elusive collaboration is especially crucial. With limited government funding, Indian universities desperately need to look into the private sector for research support.

But convincing industries to collaborate with academia? That's a whole other challenge—like explaining quantum computing to your grandma (while she knits and nods politely).

In theory, industry-academia collaboration should be the ultimate win-win. Industries get access to cutting-edge research, while universities secure much-needed funding and real-world applications for their work. In reality, however, Indian industries and universities often speak different languages (and I don't just mean Hindi vs. English). Industries are looking for quick, profitable solutions, while academic research is typically slow, methodical, and not always market-driven. What is worse is the lack of intermediary institutions that can facilitate these collaborations. Universities often lack proper technology transfer offices, and industries typically have little knowledge of the kind of research happening in academic institutions. It is like trying to form a partnership when both parties are attending two different conferences in two different cities. In the case of our country, it seems academia and industry are still missing the connecting flight to collaborative innovation.

Chapter 5: The "Global Scene"

In recent years, while Indian universities have certainly begun dipping their toes into the pool of international collaboration, they are still wearing floaties while others are doing the academic backstroke. International collaboration is no longer a luxury; it is a necessity. Yet many universities often approach it with hesitation, like someone who has been invited to a potluck but is not sure of what to bring. Indian researchers have started collaborating with international partners, but the numbers remain low compared to global research powerhouses like the U.S., China, and South Korea.

Language barriers, visa restrictions, and, most critically, a lack of institutional support are some of the main culprits, along with the aforementioned administrative blob. But the biggest challenge to international collaboration is the mindset. Many Indian universities still operate with a mentality of isolation, which might have been admirable during the days of the Green Revolution but feels somewhat outdated in an era where global collaboration drives innovation. Researchers in India often shy away from international partnerships, fearing they will not receive the same level of credit for their work or, worse, that their international collaborators will overshadow them.

Take Home—Solutions to fuel collaboration

By now, dear reader, you are probably thinking, "Enough with the problems. Let's talk solutions!" And you are absolutely right. So, let us explore how Indian universities can break free from their collaborative stagnation and embrace the future of research and innovation.

Collaboration cells

Imagine a dedicated cell within every Indian university with a single mission: facilitating collaboration. These "collaboration cells" would act as matchmakers connecting researchers from different disciplines and institutions within the country. They would also take the lead in identifying industry partners and simplifying collaborations by handling the administrative procedures on behalf of researchers. Think of them as "Matchmakers for Research," minus the swiping and awkward small talk—just smooth, seamless connections for impactful partnerships. These cells could become collaboration powerhouses, cutting through the red tape and making research partnerships as simple as booking a vacation online.

After the introduction of NEP 2020, Research and Development (R&D) Cells have been established at several universities, a step that could pave the way for such collaboration cells. But are these cells actively able to promote interdisciplinary and industry collaborations? If the answer to the question is "no," the universities can think of taking the initiative to establish dedicated collaboration cells with a single focus: to facilitate collaboration.

International collaborations

It's 2025—collaboration should not stop at national borders. With today's global challenges, from climate change to pandemics, research must be a collective international effort. Indian universities must aggressively pursue international collaborations, which can bring global perspectives and expertise to address local challenges. They should actively join or even lead international research consortia focused on tackling global issues. Through this, they can position themselves as key players in the global research ecosystem. After all, the world's top universities did not become world-class by working in isolation. They must take a cue from this and ramp up international collaborations if they want to compete on the global stage.

The introduction of NEP 2020 led to the establishment of Offices of International Affairs at many universities—a promising step towards enhancing global partnerships. It encourages Indian universities to form partnerships with foreign universities, research centers, and industries through exchange programs, joint degrees, and shared research projects. These connections with global experts aim to enhance the quality of education, introduce new ideas, and provide students with a broader perspective. However, for these offices to truly drive international collaborations, certain things must happen. They need a clear, strategic roadmap, not just a symbolic presence. They need to be equipped with the resources and expertise to navigate the complexities of international collaborations, from funding to legal requirements. Additionally, they must be empowered to cut through administrative bottlenecks. Only then can these offices carry out meaningful international partnerships.

Collaborative PhD programs

One powerful way to embed collaboration in the DNA of future researchers is through collaborative PhD programs. These programs could allow students to pursue research that spans multiple disciplines or institutions, preparing them to be the collaborative researchers of tomorrow.

How do we make this happen? PhD students could be supervised by faculty members from two different departments or institutions. This setup will not only broaden the academic experience of the student but also force collaboration at the faculty level. Universities could also design PhD programs centered around interdisciplinary research themes. For example, a program could bring together students from biology, chemistry, physics, and technology to tackle sustainability issues. NEP 2020 has proposed joint degrees, double degrees, and other initiatives aimed at encouraging academic partnerships, and it is crucial to put these ideas into action. These can enhance cross-institutional collaboration and research outcomes.

Collaborative PhD programs do not just train the researchers of tomorrow—they also create connections between faculty members and institutions and promote a culture of collaboration at every level.

Industry-academia liaisons

For industry-academia collaboration to truly flourish, we need bilingual speakers—those who can fluently speak both the language of academia and the language of business. Let's be honest: there is often a bit of a communication gap between researchers and industry professionals. On one side, we have academics meticulously working on theories, lab experiments, and publishing papers. On the other side, we have industries focused on marketable products, profit margins, and quarterly returns. What we need are industry-academia liaisons, who are dedicated professionals within universities and understand both worlds. These liaisons would work closely with industries to understand their immediate and long-term needs and communicate to academia how their research could offer solutions to these industry challenges. They can also help industries see the potential long-term benefits of supporting more fundamental or exploratory research.

In essence, they would be the diplomats of the research world, fluent in both technical jargon and corporate lingo. These liaisons could even help negotiate the thorny issues around intellectual property rights and patent ownership, which often throw a wrench into collaborative efforts. This approach is similar to what research universities in the U.S. and Europe do. They establish dedicated, industry-focused offices to handle technology transfer and ensure that lab breakthroughs actually reach the market. This makes collaboration a smoother, more rewarding process for both parties.

Create funding pools for collaboration

Collaboration thrives when it is financially supported. Researchers are far more likely to team up when they know there is money behind it. So, how do we fund this collaborative utopia? By creating funding pools specifically for collaborative research projects. Think of it as venture capital but for knowledge. These funding pools could be created from philanthropic donations, alumni contributions, endowments and trust funds, public-private partnerships, corporate sponsorships, other private-sector investments, or even crowdfunding for research. Attaching financial incentives to collaboration will motivate researchers to actively seek partners from different disciplines or universities. After all, nothing fuels the research engine like funding.

Shared research infrastructure

Equipment envy is real, folks. One university might have a state-of-the-art electron microscope, while another might have cutting-edge software for data analysis. Instead of hoarding resources, why not share? Universities can make expensive, specialized equipment accessible to more researchers by promoting shared research infrastructure. This approach would significantly reduce costs while boosting the quality and quantity of research being done. Sharing infrastructure does not just make financial sense—it also naturally encourages collaboration as researchers from different institutions come together to use the same equipment. While NEP 2020 advocates for the sharing of research and teaching infrastructure through the clustering of colleges and the formation of consortiums, this vision must be turned into reality through practical implementation.

Recognizing collaboration

If you want people to collaborate, you need to make it worth their while. One effective way to do this is by recognizing and rewarding collaboration. Universities can create annual awards for the best collaborative research projects. These could come with perks such as cash prizes, recognition at university events, or even additional research funding. Nothing motivates like the chance to have some extra funding and a shiny trophy. Faculty members should be rewarded for collaborative efforts, not just individual achievements. In addition, researchers often hesitate to collaborate because they fear not receiving enough credit for their work. Clear guidelines on co-authorship credits can help resolve these concerns and ensure that everyone gets their fair share of recognition. Creating a culture that acknowledges and rewards collaboration will inspire researchers to actively pursue partnerships and make working together the new norm.

The Future of Research in India—A Vision Build on Collaboration

The secret sauce of collaboration in Indian academia seems to have gone missing. The future of research and innovation in Indian universities hinges on how well they can collaborate. Collaboration isn't just a buzzword—it is the key to solving complex global challenges and driving innovation. Our universities possess the talent, ambition, and intellectual capital to become leaders in global research. However, to realize this potential, they have to embrace collaboration at every level—from research infrastructure to PhD programs and from industry partnerships to international consortia. This approach will not only enhance research output but it will also help secure their place in the global academic landscape. So, dear reader, let's dream big. Let's imagine a future where Indian universities work together seamlessly, where interdisciplinary teams are the norm, and where research knows no borders—only breakthroughs.

Disclaimer: *The names of subjects, fields, and any specific references here have been randomly picked from the chaotic cosmos of academia and bear no resemblance to actual individuals, institutions, or areas of study (unless, of course, you insist on seeing yourself in them). In that case,* *the resemblance is purely coincidental and entirely your problem. My sole mission is to shed light on the tangled web of collaboration in Indian academia, spark a little reflection (and maybe a chuckle or two), and promote dialogue (without pointing fingers). So, read on, reflect, and relax.*

When Analog Minds Meet Digital Dreams: Generational Clash in Research

It was a busy Monday morning at the National Institute of Fundamental Science (NIFS), one of India's oldest and most respected science institutes. You would expect groundbreaking discoveries here every other day, right? But ask any scientist at NIFS, and they will tell you the real daily challenge: dealing with never-ending file movements and the tricky art of working across generations. Meet Dr. Atul Patel, a veteran biochemist with over 30 years of experience. He swears by handwritten notes, old-school experiments, and hours hunched over test tubes. For Dr. Patel, "real science" happens in the lab, hands-on. "Computers are great, but they are no substitute for the real thing," he would say, waving around a worn-out paper like a badge of honor. On the other end, there is Dr. Ananya Mehta, a young, tech-savvy computational biologist who practically lives on her laptop. With data-analysis software and Python skills, she sees research as one big data puzzle just waiting to be solved digitally. To her, efficiency is key, and who needs hours at the lab bench when a few lines of code can do the job?

So folks, here we are—a standoff between the "old-school" and "new-school" scientists. While Dr. Patel sees the digital shift as cutting corners, Dr. Mehta sees it as a step into the future. This is the story of how Dr. Patel and Dr. Mehta learned to work together—or, more accurately, learned not to get in each other's way while trying to complete a research project. And somewhere along the line, they discovered that maybe there were things both generations could learn from each other to bridge the vast chasm between them. And NIFS? Well, it's caught in the middle, trying to balance both approaches and wondering if its next big discovery will simply be getting everyone on the same page.

Chapter 1: The "Setup"

One fine day, the director of the institute announced a new collaborative research project on a genetic disorder found in certain rural communities in India. This project, he said, needed the "wisdom of experience" and the "power of innovation." In other words, Dr. Patel and Dr. Mehta were in charge, whether they liked it or not. Maybe the director thought their combined expertise would make magic, or maybe he just wanted to give them both a wake-up call. Dr. Patel eyed his young partner with suspicion. He had seen too many impatient, tech-driven researchers cut corners that, in his view, missed the real point of science. "They don't make scientists like they used to," he mused. Meanwhile, Ananya managed a polite smile, but her thoughts were less friendly. "Why go through all these time-consuming manual experiments?" she wondered. "A few simulations, some machine learning, and problem solved." And so, the stage was set: a battle of old-school grit versus digital dreams, each scientist doubting the other's methods but bound to work together. At NIFS, everyone watched, half-expecting this project's first "discovery" to be who would cave first.

Chapter 2: The "Paperwork Barrier"

Their first meeting was a sight to behold: Dr. Patel, 15 minutes early, lugged in a mountain of old lab reports plastered with sticky notes. Dr. Mehta arrived exactly on time, armed only with her laptop and a polished slide deck. Just as they began, in came Mrs. Ghosh from Admin with an announcement. "Before you start," she said cheerfully, "you will need approvals from the Biosafety Committee, Internal Review Board, Finance Committee, and, of course, the Human Ethics Committee."

Dr. Mehta's face fell. "How long will that take?"

"Oh, not too long!" Mrs. Ghosh said with a proud smile. "Maybe three to six months if you are lucky!"

Dr. Patel leaned over with a smirk. "Welcome to Indian science," he whispered, clearly amused by her shocked expression.

Chapter 3: The "Lab Scene"

After they finally got through the endless approval process, Dr. Patel and Dr. Mehta could dive into the actual science. Dr. Mehta suggested they kick things off with a wide-ranging data analysis, using large-scale simulations to figure out which genes to target in their experiments. Dr. Patel frowned and muttered, "All these fancy algorithms… What is the point if you don't get your hands dirty? Science is not about guessing the results; it is about proving them with real evidence." He waved at her laptop like it was some alien artifact. "Back in my day, we didn't need all this coding nonsense."

"Back in your day," Dr. Mehta shot back sweetly, "we didn't even know the structure of DNA."

Dr. Patel coughed, caught off guard. "Fair point," he admitted.

But it sparked an idea for Dr. Mehta. Maybe they could blend their methods—use simulations to make educated guesses and then have Dr. Patel validate the findings in the lab. He hesitated but eventually agreed.

Then came the funding hiccup. Just as they were starting their preliminary tests, Dr. Patel received the dreaded email: "Your current funding financial year ends this month. Please apply for an extension or look for alternative grants."

"Alternative grants?" Dr. Mehta exclaimed, exasperated. "Isn't this project supposed to be important? How can we keep moving without money?"

Dr. Patel shrugged. "Welcome to the reality of Indian research. Back in my day, we sometimes paid for our experiments ourselves."

Dr. Mehta blinked. "That's crazy!"

"Science isn't free," he said with a wistful smile.

They both sighed, feeling the weight of their situation. Dr. Mehta, being the tech whiz she was, quickly found some crowdfunding platforms for science projects. "It's a bit unconventional," she said, "but maybe we can convince people to support something meaningful?"

As they moved forward with their research, it became obvious that their thought processes were like oil and water. Dr. Patel, a veteran researcher with decades of experience, was set in his traditional ways. He prided himself on his careful, hands-on approach, which had led him to many successes. On the other hand, Dr. Mehta's methods were all about speed and automation. She effortlessly ran complex simulations on her laptop, solved numbers in minutes, and trusted software predictions like they were sacred vows.

Dr. Patel often watched her work with a skeptical eye. "Do you really believe those results?" he asked one afternoon as he peered at her computer screen, where a flashy genetic map was glowing. "Back in my day, we would spend days or even weeks verifying something like that in the lab. There is no shortcut in science."

Dr. Mehta rolled her eyes, trying to be polite. "Dr. Patel, if we can save time without losing accuracy, why not? These simulations can uncover patterns and data faster than any manual experiment ever could."

Dr. Patel shook his head. "But the issue is, these new methods can give you answers without real understanding. Science is not about rushing to results; it is about grasping each step along the way."

He had a point, and Dr. Mehta knew it. The careful ways of the old-school scientists meant they rarely missed the little things. Back in their day, a single experiment could take months, which made them appreciate each step in the research process. For them, those long, detailed stages were like a ritual, showing the true dedication of a scientist. To Dr. Patel, research was like cooking a traditional dish that needed hours of simmering to bring out the flavors. Anything quicker felt like "instant science"—nice to look at but lacking real substance.

But sometimes, Dr. Patel's mindset became more of a hurdle than a badge of honor. His unwillingness to accept new technology often dragged out processes that Dr. Mehta knew could be done in a fraction of the time. For example, Dr. Patel insisted on manually recording his experimental data in dusty handwritten logbooks, while Dr. Mehta loved using cloud tools that let her access her work anytime, anywhere. When she suggested he digitize his notes for better data management, Dr. Patel chuckled and said, "Who needs that when you have pen and paper? The computer won't help you remember the little details."

"Or it just might," she muttered under her breath.

It wasn't that Dr. Patel was completely against new technology; he just struggled to see how it could ever match the carefulness and depth of traditional methods. To him, the digital approach felt too "easy," even though Dr. Mehta often got results that were just as good and reliable. The truth was their different styles surprisingly complemented each other, but convincing Dr. Patel to see that was a challenge. This stubborn mindset was common among the old-school scientists at NIFS. Many of them, like Dr. Patel, held onto their methods, not just out of habit but also pride. They had done groundbreaking research, trained countless students, and built their careers on these traditional approaches. The common saying was, "If it has worked for decades, why change?"

Dr. Mehta understood where he was coming from, but she couldn't help but feel frustrated at times. "Just because something is new doesn't mean it cuts corners," she told him one day. "We can keep our accuracy, but these new methods let us explore more ideas in less time." In her mind, there was no reason to hold onto old ways just because they were "proven." The world had changed, and science needed to change too. If we want to make real progress, we have to embrace new tools, even if that means letting go of some traditional mindset.

And to her surprise, over time, Dr. Patel seemed to come around to this idea, little by little. In the end, both realized they had valuable insights to offer. Dr. Patel's carefulness balanced Dr. Mehta's speed, while her excitement for new technology brought a fresh twist to his tried-and-tested methods. Together, they found a middle ground—a way to respect the past while welcoming innovation. And perhaps, that was the secret to bridging the generation gap in Indian science.

Chapter 4: The "Breakthrough"

After months of working together, Dr. Mehta and Dr. Patel finally made some real progress. Dr. Mehta suggested they present their findings at an international conference to get some attention for their project. Dr. Patel sighed dramatically. "Ah, conferences. In my day, we only presented once every few years. Now, it's all about flashy slides and trendy topics. They even make you bring digital posters! Back in my day, we did everything by hand."

"And today, you can reach a global audience from your laptop," Dr. Mehta shot back. "Think of the impact! Don't you want the world to see our research?"

"Fair point," he admitted, though it clearly pained him. Dr. Patel realized that maybe it was time to embrace some change.

Finally, after months of mixing Dr. Mehta's tech-savvy methods combined with Dr. Patel's careful experiments, they made a breakthrough that even surprised them. Their findings not only shed new light on the genetic disorder but also hinted at a potential treatment pathway that nobody had thought of before. The director was thrilled and immediately encouraged them to publish. Their project became a shining example at NIFS, proving that the wisdom of age and the energy of youth could lead to amazing discoveries.

When their paper was finally published, Dr. Patel proudly handed Dr. Mehta a handwritten letter that read, "In Science, No Experiment Is Truly Alone." It was a thank you and a gentle reminder that the best discoveries often happen somewhere in the middle—when old and new come together.

Take Home-Uniting generations for a brighter scientific future

Dr. Patel and Dr. Mehta's journey was not just a clash of generational styles—it was a front-row seat to the *uniquely Indian* challenges researchers face. From administrative delays that make grant applications feel like epic quests to funding struggles that turn scientists into financial acrobats, these hurdles have been part of Indian science forever. And honestly, it's high time we did something about them.

So, here is a look at the quirks and troubles haunting India's scientific world—served with a healthy dose of sarcasm, a list of our all-time favorite headaches, and maybe a sprinkle of possible fixes. Because if we can't laugh at the madness, what's even the point? Let's call out these issues and see if we can turn this glorious mess into something that actually works.

Generation gap is not a battle; it's a band

Ah, the generational divide in Indian science—it's a gap so wide you could drive a truck through it. On one side, we have our beloved Old-Gen scientists, clinging to methods they perfected before the internet was even a twinkle in a tech nerd's eye. On the other hand, the Next-Gen researchers are ready to hit fast-forward, armed with gadgets and apps that can calculate things faster than you can say "quantum physics." But instead of viewing each other as adversaries in a mad scientist showdown, what if they recognize they could be more like a rock band? Let's be honest: every great band needs a little wisdom from the seasoned guitarist who has been around since the days of cassette tapes.

Imagine a world where Old-Gen and Next-Gen scientists are jamming together in harmony instead of glaring across the lab like it's the last piece of rasogulla at a conference. Instead of the usual "Get off my lawn" mentality, why not create regular forums where they can meet, swap ideas, and (dare I say) share a laugh? Think of joint research projects that capitalize on both youth and experience: the seniors bring their sage-like stability, while the young guns infuse fresh energy and maybe a dash of questionable TikTok trends into the mix.

Picture this: a lab where the Old-Gen scientist, equipped with the instincts of a seasoned detective, helps troubleshoot the Next-Gen's wild ideas while the youngsters whip up solutions that make the Old-Gen's heads spin faster than a centrifuge. Teamwork makes the research dream work, and who knows? Maybe the result will be a hit song in the scientific community instead of a lonely ballad of old methods and new dreams! So, let's grab our lab coats, tune our instruments, and make some scientific music together! After all, when different generations collaborate, the symphony of science becomes richer and more vibrant!

Streamlining administrative processes

Indian research administration, where brilliant ideas wait endlessly in line for hours, begging for approval stamps and signing forms in triplicate! Forget lab coats; Indian researchers might as well trade them for tracksuits and gear up for endurance marathons! Applying for a grant?

You better start six months early because approvals move at a pace that makes snails look like Ferraris. And if you are trying to import specialized equipment, get cozy—you might receive it just in time for your retirement party.

Now, imagine a magical India where every institution has a "Scientific Express Lane." Picture a team of administrators who actually know how to handle paperwork, zipping through grants, travel approvals, and purchase orders like Olympic relay runners. And let's not forget about going digital—how about e-signatures? It's not 1990 anymore, and we are definitely tired of wasting precious research hours chasing down signatures from every Tom, Dick, and Office Clerk. It is high time to bring the administration into the 21st century and stop making researchers feel like they are stuck in a never-ending line for a rollercoaster ride!

Restructure conferences

Indian conferences are famous for their incredible catering, and who can resist the endless chai and samosas? The steaming high teas and lavish buffets are often the highlight of the event. But imagine instead of rows of chairs facing a screen, let's envision "Conference Labs"—small, interactive setups where researchers can dive into real-world challenges together. We could create engaging labs where senior and junior scientists share perspectives while actually doing hands-on tasks instead of just sipping another cup of chai.

Now, picture ending the day with relaxed, structured, but informal networking lounges, where young researchers are encouraged to lead discussions while seasoned scientists sprinkle in their wisdom. We could even have fun brainstorming competitions or breakout groups where every voice is genuinely heard. Imagine combining our traditional hospitality with real collaboration opportunities! Let's create spaces for scientists to connect. After all, it's time to make conferences more about working together and less about calorie counts!

The Future of Research in India—Together, Easier, Faster, Better

Through their journey, Dr. Patel and Dr. Mehta realized that for Indian science to thrive, it's not just about more labs or fancier machines. It is about creating a culture where each generation respects each other's strengths. Imagine an India where scientists spend more time discovering and less time applying for permissions, where interdisciplinary projects flourish, and where conferences spark real innovation. With these changes, Indian science could be on track to world-class standards.

Maybe, just maybe, the next Dr. Patel and Dr. Mehta won't have to climb piles of paperwork, juggle inconsistent funding, or sit through interminable PowerPoints to make a difference. Instead, they will have the tools, funding, and support they need to transform their ideas into breakthroughs that put Indian science on the global map. And with NEP 2020 in play, the universities and institutions are allowed to develop a flexible, multidisciplinary, comprehensive education system that could actually make this dream a reality. Who would not want a brighter future where science is actually fun and not just a rigid mindset stuck in the past?

Disclaimer: *The story of Dr. Patel and Dr. Mehta is entirely fictional (seriously!). Any resemblance to real scientists alive is purely coincidental. The arguments between old-school and new-school science are meant for laughs, not fights in the lab. No egos, lab tools, or computers were hurt in the process. And if this feels a bit too real, maybe it's time to ask why reality feels like satire. Read with a smile and a little self-reflection!*

Finding Creative Solutions in a Low-Budget Lab

Dr. Aditya Iyer, freshly graduated with a Ph.D., had big dreams. After years of stress and late nights, he was finally ready to make his mark in science. In his mind, he was a mix of Einstein and Curie, but with a distinctly Indian twist. So, when he finally got his own lab, his hopes were higher than the mountains. "Finally, a place to make scientific history," he thought. But as he stepped into his new lab, reality hit harder than a power outage during the summer heat.

The lab was, in a word, "minimalist." The equipment looked older than his grandmother's spice grinder. His lab bench seemed like it had survived multiple fires, and who knows what those old, dusty glass bottles on the shelf held? Maybe it was holy water; maybe it was poison. The single, flickering tube light above him made the place look like a haunted house scene. He took a deep breath. "Well," he muttered, "at least the electricity is there."

The biggest "surprise" was the microscope. He approached it respectfully, but as he leaned closer, he realized it wasn't a microscope at all; it was a dusty, ancient relic that may have been a microscope in the

1960s. Squinting through it, he hoped he could see… anything, really. Aditya took a deep breath, trying to reassure himself. "This is just a minor setback. I don't need fancy equipment to make groundbreaking discoveries?" he thought. "This lab might be a disaster, but I am still a genius. Right?"

Chapter 1: The "Equipment Meltdown"

In his first few weeks, Aditya's excitement for his new lab slowly turned into a strange mix of fear and dark humor. What he had thought was a "research facility" was beginning to feel more like a high-budget horror film scene or, at best, a scrapyard someone had optimistically labeled "Lab." Instruments were scattered everywhere, like ancient fossils of old science experiments. Some had such a thick coat of rust you could almost call it "science archaeology." The equipment seemed to be sending him a message: "Retirement is overdue."

The centrifuge, a key player in almost any chemistry lab, was the first thing he noticed. It looked harmless, with a faint shine hidden beneath layers of dust. "Ah, finally, something I can use!" he thought with the kind of hope reserved for lottery winners. He carefully placed his sample inside, pressed the button, and… nothing. He gave it a little tap, then a solid thump. And finally, a desperate slap. With a cranky noise, it whirred to life, spun once, wobbled like it was going to faint, then let out a soft sigh and died completely. Aditya stood there holding a sad beaker of sediment, looking into it and feeling nothing but pure, distilled disappointment.

But Aditya wasn't the type to give up easily. "Who needs a fancy centrifuge?" he thought, laughing at the very idea of functional equipment. Inspiration struck when he saw his nephew's spinning top lying around. Why not use that? He grabbed it, tied some microfuge tubes to it with rubber bands, and spun it by hand. "If I spin fast enough," he figured, "it's basically the same thing as a centrifuge. Science doesn't care about brand names!" He leaned in to watch the samples slowly separate and felt proud of himself. "There," he said proudly, " this is jugaad science at its best."

And that was just the beginning.

Next, he looked at the Bunsen burner—a basic piece of equipment for any self-respecting lab. This particular burner looked as if it had last produced a flame around the same time the dinosaurs roamed. No matter what he tried, it wouldn't light up. Aditya used every trick he could think of: he twisted the knobs, poked it with a paper clip, and even whispered a little prayer. But nothing worked. So, he did what any clever scientist would do: he went home, grabbed an old gas stove from his mom's kitchen, and carried it to the lab.

Now, this wasn't just any stove; it was a 20-year-old piece of junk that had probably survived a few wars and was about as delicate as a bulldozer. But it worked. Squatting on the floor with his makeshift "Bunsen burner," he lit the flame and said, "Who needs style when you have passion?" He even came up with a tagline for it: "Made in India, Tested by Frustration." It had a certain charm to it, he thought, as he adjusted the flame intensity with his mom's trusty stove knobs.

When his colleagues saw him doing science experiments on an old gas stove, they couldn't help but laugh. "Is this a lab or a roadside chai stall?" they teased. But Aditya, never one to miss a chance to joke back, just smiled and replied, "Science is about adaptability, my friends. If Edison had a gas stove, he would have used it too!" His friends didn't know whether to admire his creativity or call an electrician.

And so, Dr. Aditya's lab started transforming, bit by bit, into a workshop of improvised science.

Chapter 2: The "Art of Recycling and Reinvention"

Funding was as rare as fresh air during Parali season in Delhi, so getting new chemicals for his experiments was simply out of the question. Instead, Aditya took on the role of a master scavenger, roaming nearby labs like a hungry squirrel gathering nuts for winter. Each expired chemical he collected had its own quirky backstory—some came from a lab that had shut down five years ago, while others were so old that their labels had peeled off and vanished into oblivion. But hey, Aditya thought, chemistry is chemistry, right? A little dust never hurt anyone!

He quickly earned the nickname "MacGyver of Science" as he turned everyday items into research tools. When he found himself in need of pipettes, he didn't hesitate. Instead, he raided a roadside tea stall for plastic straws and paired them with a leaky old dropper for good measure. Petri dishes? No problem! He simply fashioned them from disposable plastic plates. Syringes became his precision tools, and he even taped his smartphone to a toy microscope to capture "high-resolution" images that would make any professional lab technician weep.

However, Aditya's crowning achievement was his own version of a fume hood (a must-have for any chemistry lab), yet typically a luxury item he couldn't afford. Armed with an old exhaust fan and a roll of duct tape, he created what he called the "Lab Safety Zone" in the corner of his workspace. The final product was a drafty, noisy contraption that looked more like a homemade pizza oven than a legitimate fume hood. "Fume Hood 2.0," he proudly called it, demonstrating how it could blow smoke into the neighboring department, thereby keeping his own workspace free of the worst fumes. If nothing else, Aditya was proving that in the world of science, creativity could turn dire situations into a recipe for success!

Chapter 3: The "Power of Jugaad Science"

Aditya quickly realized he wasn't alone in his quest for creative solutions in research. Soon, he found a small group of fellow scientists who were navigating similar challenges. They affectionately called themselves "The Jugaad Scientists," and every month, they gathered over cups of steaming chai for brainstorming sessions that often turned into lively discussions filled with laughter. This was no ordinary meetup; it was an underground network of scientists who were determined to make do with what they had, sharing ideas and strategies for innovative problem-solving. During these gatherings, they shared ideas on how to make lab equipment from everyday items. For instance, a discarded refrigerator, once forgotten in a corner, transformed into an incubator that kept their cultures at just the right temperature. An old washing machine drum, which had long been out of service, was repurposed into an agitator for mixing solutions. They even found a way to use a dusty overhead projector left behind by the library as a light source for plant growth experiments. For Aditya, each invention proved that science did not require the latest, most expensive tools. Instead, it thrived on creativity, adaptability, and a readiness to embrace the unexpected.

This group was not just about laughs; it became a vital support system. When experiments failed or frustrations mounted, they came together to motivate each other, reminding one another that setbacks were just part of the journey. There is nothing quite like the joy of celebrating small victories together (like the thrill of getting a pH meter to work after a clever fix with a glue gun and spare wires). In their shared struggles and successes, Aditya found inspiration and a sense of belonging, proving that collaboration and community could light the path forward in even the toughest of times.

Chapter 4: The "Publication of Findings"

Finally, after years of struggle and improvisation, Aditya had collected enough data to submit a research paper. Sure, the experiments were held together by rubber bands and a lot of hope, but the results were genuine. They might not have been groundbreaking discoveries that would change the face of science, but they were solid enough to contribute to his field. And most importantly, the work was uniquely his. In the acknowledgments, he cheekily noted, "This work would not have been possible without generous help from family kitchenware, neighborhood electronics, and a strong faith in jugaad." It was a humorous nod to his unconventional methods.

The moment he hit "submit," Aditya felt a mix of excitement and nervousness wash over him. It was as if he had just climbed Mount Everest, wearing nothing but a pair of slippers and clutching a handful of peanuts. He realized he was finally taking a step into the world of published research, a milestone he had worked hard to reach despite the odds stacked against him. Aditya understood that this paper represented more than just data; it was a testament to his resilience and creativity. He had overcome obstacles that would have made many others give up. As he sat back, he felt a sense of pride in his journey, knowing he had earned his place in the scientific community, no matter how limited his resources were.

In the days that followed, he couldn't help but smile at the thought of his paper making its way into the hands of readers. Who knew? Perhaps his story would inspire other scientists facing similar challenges to embrace their own journeys and innovate with what they have, proving that science thrives on creativity and determination.

Take Home—Determination, resilience, and resourcefulness

Looking back on his journey, Aditya realized he learned more than just science; he learned what it means to be a true scientist. In the world of research, fancy tools are nice, but being strong and resourceful is what really matters. This

is exactly what NEP 2020 aims to achieve—developing adaptable, resilient, and practical thinking. It focuses on building critical thinking, problem-solving, and creative learning. Aditya showed all of these qualities. Even though his lab did not have the latest equipment like some well-funded labs, he showed the self-reliance that the policy encourages. His story reminds us that the best tool for a researcher is their mind, and sometimes, the biggest discoveries come from a strong desire to learn, not from expensive equipment. In India, where research budgets are often modest, Aditya's journey is one that many scientists can relate to. Here are a few important lessons from his story:

Innovation over investment

When resources are limited, being innovative becomes essential. Aditya didn't let his old equipment stop him; instead, he turned his challenges into opportunities to think outside the box and find clever solutions.

Teamwork makes the dream work

The support he received from his fellow "Jugaad Scientists" was incredibly helpful. NEP 2020 encourages collaboration across different fields and institutions, and Aditya's journey demonstrates that sharing knowledge and having a sense of community can help everyone achieve more than they could alone.

Patience and persistence

In research, things rarely go as planned, especially when working with a low budget. Aditya's determination to keep going, even when it felt like everything was against him, showcases the resilience that NEP 2020 aims to nurture in students and researchers alike.

A mindset of curiosity

At the heart of all research lies curiosity. The story of Aditya serves as a reminder that while having good equipment and funding is helpful, it is ultimately the mindset of the researcher that drives discoveries and innovation.

The Future of Research in India—A Path to Innovation and Growth

In many ways, Aditya embodies the principles of NEP 2020. He showed that even though the research environment may come with its own challenges, limitations can spark creativity and a strong spirit for science. Research is really about having the right mindset and attitude, not just about having the latest and greatest tools. And with that, Aditya continued his journey, and his lab of jugaad grew brighter with each discovery. This reminds us all that in research, the only limit is our imagination and our willingness to explore new ideas.

The future of Indian research is bright, especially in universities. As universities change to meet the needs of a fast-moving world, they are starting to see challenges as chances for innovation. Research in India is becoming more collaborative, with universities encouraging teamwork across different fields and promoting a culture of creativity. And the NEP 2020 is playing its part in this change. This new approach allows students and researchers to try new things and explore beyond traditional limits. Universities must focus on developing a curious mindset instead of just memorizing facts and prepare graduates to solve real-world problems with fresh ideas. They must also work to connect research with local communities and ensure that new discoveries address local needs. This will not only improve the quality of research but also strengthen the relationship between universities and society. Encouraging resilience and creativity can make the future of Indian science very promising. Researchers have the ability to turn challenges into opportunities, making India to become a leader in global scientific innovation. The road ahead looks bright, powered by imagination and a strong desire to learn.

Disclaimer: *This story is mostly made up and meant to be a fun take on science done with limited resources. If it reminds you of real labs or people, that is just a coincidence (or maybe not!) Please don't actually use toy microscopes, duct-taped fume hoods, or expired chemicals unless you have a PhD in Jugaadology. Always put safety first—unless you are Aditya, then just hope the fumes go to the other room.*

The Night Owl Researchers

In a lively research lab hidden near the ghats of the Ganges, a unique group of researchers came alive when most people were dreaming of distant shores and starry nights. This lab, filled with colorful sticky notes and messy drawings, was home to the "Night Owl Researchers"—the champions of late-night science!

The night air was thick with the intense smell of coffee and the sound of the keyboard clacking. These researchers didn't just stay up late; they thrived on it, and were fueled by two essential ingredients: way too much caffeine and an insatiable curiosity about the mysteries of life.

Dr. Vidya, the biochemist with hair that looked like it had survived a tornado, was always cooking up crazy ideas. Then there was Rahul, the physicist, who thought quantum mechanics could solve all his problems (even his sleep issues). And let's not forget Maya, the biologist, who talked to her petri dishes as if they were her pets, claiming they were just misunderstood little creatures, much like her. Together, they made an odd but brilliant team, conducting hilarious experiments and sharing late-night Maggi. Who needs sleep when you have midnight breakthroughs and the joy of slightly crazy ideas? In their world, the best discoveries were made between sips of coffee and bursts of laughter!

Chapter 1: The "Call of Curiosity"

As the clock struck midnight, Vidya was bent over her lab bench, squinting at a mass spectrometer like it was a magic portal to another dimension. "If we just adjust the enzyme concentration, we might finally figure out why my coffee never tastes as good as my mom's!" she exclaimed, sounding as confident as someone who hasn't slept in days.

"I think you might be onto something, Vidya," Rahul replied, rubbing his tired eyes. "Maybe the coffee molecules are just in a state of existential crisis!" He chuckled at his own joke, which was hilarious only to a physicist at midnight.

Between bouts of inspiration, they shared stories about their previous late-night adventures. Like the time Rahul mistakenly mixed up his lab samples with his dinner leftovers. "I will never look at paneer tikka the same way again!" he said, shaking his head, still horrified.

Each member of the Night Owl Researchers had their own ridiculous tale, like Maya's infamous "Bacterial Dance-Off," where she somehow convinced her teammates to dance to Bollywood songs while conducting an experiment. "We discovered that certain strains of E. coli respond surprisingly well to 'Badtameez Dil!'" she declared with pride, as if they had just made a groundbreaking discovery.

Amid laughter and sarcasm, they enjoy in the chaos of their late-night research. Here, in the dim glow of computer screens and flickering fluorescent lights, creativity flourished like a stubborn weed. For them, every midnight hour was a chance to unravel the mysteries of science, one wild idea at a time. They didn't need sleep; they had coffee, laughs, the crazy joy of working together, and being the Night Owl Researchers!

Chapter 2: The "Midnight Maggi"

As the night dragged on, the warm smell of coffee filled the lab, mixing with the delightful scent of Maggi. This was the real fuel of the Night Owl Researchers. Vidya had her own special coffee recipe, rumored to have magical powers that enhanced creativity.

"Is it caffeine, or is it your 'secret ingredient' that is making me see things?" Maya asked, looking at her mug as if it might start dancing. "I swear my mug just winked at me!"

"Maybe that is a sign you should name it and start a new science called 'Mug-ology!'" Rahul joked, chuckling at the idea.

They all laughed, but soon, their giggles turned into big yawns. "Alright, team, break time!" Vidya declared, reaching for their ever-reliable snack stash. "What do we have left? More aloo chips or the last bit of samosa?"

"I will take anything with the highest carbohydrate content!" Rahul said eagerly. "We need all the energy we can get to fight off the 'black hole' of sleep that is trying to suck us in."

Maya nodded, eyes half-closed. "I cannot believe we are actually discussing our food choices like it is a science experiment. 'Which snack will save our sanity?'"

"Aloo chips or samosa—this is the real research," Vidya replied, grinning. "Who knew that midnight snacks would be the key to our discoveries?"

With a mix of snacks and laughter, they fueled their late-night adventures, proving that for the Night Owl Researchers, food was just as important as science. After all, how could they uncover the mysteries of life without a little carbs and caffeine?

Chapter 3: The "Delirious Discoveries"

As the night began to creep in, the lab was buzzing with an unusual kind of energy—one that definitely would not make it into any scientific journals. The Night Owl Researchers were deep in discussion about their latest groundbreaking project: a study on the "Effects of Sleep Deprivation on Creative Problem Solving in the Context of Indian Cuisine."

"Let's be real here," Maya said, laughter bubbling out of her. "We are basically experts at this! The less sleep we get, the more brilliant our ideas seem to become! Like my theory about why dosa batter never ferments properly."

"Ah, yes, the infamous dosa dilemma," Rahul said, grinning like a kid in a candy store. "Maybe the batter is just as tired as we are and refuses to rise to the occasion! It probably wants a nice nap too!"

Their laughter filled the lab, echoing off the walls like the best kind of symphony. In the middle of all this hilarity, Vidya's eyes lit up with a spark of inspiration. "What if we crafted a hypothesis that links sleep deprivation to spontaneous bursts of culinary creativity? It could explain why late-night chefs come up with such wild and delicious dishes!"

With every ridiculous suggestion, they scribbled notes, their ideas getting sillier by the minute. The air was thick with caffeine and creativity, and amidst the laughter and absurdity, a breakthrough popped up like a well-risen dosa. "What if we merged our love for science with our passion for food?" Vidya mused, her mind racing. "We could write a cookbook that explains scientific principles through recipes!"

Maya's eyes widened with excitement. "I can see it now! 'The Quantum Kitchen: Recipes for Entangled Flavors'—it will be a bestseller!" She jumped up from her seat, waving her arms dramatically as if she were presenting an award-winning idea.

"Of course! We could have chapters on 'Molecular Gastronomy for the Home Cook' and 'How to Make Your Paneer Absolutely Unbreakable!'" Rahul added, practically bouncing in his chair. "I mean, who wouldn't want to learn how to use quantum physics to improve their aloo paratha-making skills?"

"Exactly! And think about it, we could even have a section on 'Sleep-Deprived Recipes' for those late-night cravings," Vidya said, her excitement contagious. "You know, things like 'Instant Maggi Noodles with a Dash of Desperation!'"

As they continued to brainstorm, the ideas kept flowing like the never-ending cups of coffee. They talked about how they could illustrate scientific principles in a way that even their sleep-deprived brains could understand—maybe a recipe for 'Coffee that Will Keep You Awake' could explain the chemistry behind caffeine!

With every chuckle and every silly idea, the Night Owl Researchers found themselves on the verge of creating something truly unique. It was not just a cookbook; it was a celebration of the wild, wonderful, and sometimes absurd intersection of science and food. Who knew that their late-night delirium could lead to such culinary genius? As they prepared to wrap up their brainstorming session, they realized that they had not only entertained themselves but also found a new and exciting project that combined their passions.

With their eyes twinkling and their minds racing, they were ready to take the culinary world by storm—one sleep-deprived recipe at a time!

Chapter 4: The "Eternal Struggle of Science vs. Sleep"

As dawn crept over the ghats of the Ganges, a thick fog of fatigue blanketed in the lab, making the Night Owl Researchers feel like they were wading through the river's sluggish morning mist. With half-closed eyes, they found themselves caught in an epic battle between their relentless thirst for knowledge and the irresistible pull to give in to sleep.

"Remember the golden rule of research: sleep is for the weak!" Rahul proclaimed dramatically, raising his coffee mug as a trophy. The irony was not lost on him, especially since he was practically sipping liquid exhaustion.

"I don't think I can keep my eyes open any longer," Maya confessed, her head bobbing as she fought to stay awake. "Maybe we should set up a sleep experiment? I would like to find out how quickly I can dream about working on protein dynamics while snoozing in a lab chair."

"Don't forget to account for the effects of the lab's fluorescent lights," Vidya chimed in, already drifting off as she spoke. "They could be the secret to unlocking the mysteries of the universe—or at least the key to some really weird dreams."

The trio erupted into laughter again, their giggles echoing off the lab walls, but it didn't last long. Just then, their phones buzzed loudly, breaking the moment. They had a group chat aptly named "The Owl Nest," where they traded the latest research articles and shared hilarious memes about their shared love for sleepless nights.

"This group is scientifically engineered to keep us awake!" Rahul announced with a dramatic flair, scrolling through the messages. He paused at a meme of a cartoon owl with bloodshot eyes, captioned, "Sleep is for the weak!"

"Brilliant! That is exactly how I feel!" Maya said, laughing, though she was struggling to keep her own eyes from closing.

But despite the relentless buzz of notifications, the thick cloud of fatigue refused to lift. The thought of collapsing into their lab chairs for just a few stolen minutes of sleep grew stronger with every passing second, like a siren call they were struggling to resist.

"Maybe we should just give in," Vidya suggested, her voice barely a whisper. "We could set up a 'Sleep Research Facility' right here in the lab! I can already see it: 'Testing the Effects of Mid-Morning Naps on Research Productivity.'"

"Hey, that could be a great grant proposal!" Rahul joked, rubbing his eyes vigorously. "I'm sure they would love to fund the 'Napping Scientists Initiative.'"

Maya snickered. "Yeah, they will say, 'Sleep is essential for productive research, but don't let that interfere with your caffeine intake!'"

As they joked and laughed, the tiredness started to catch up with them. Their eyes felt heavy, and each minute seemed to drag on. Eventually, the laughter faded, and a deep sigh filled the room.

"Alright, it's time," Maya said, moving her chair closer to her desk. "Let's embrace our inner owls and take a quick nap. Science will still be here when we wake up, right?" With that, they adjusted their chairs, settled in, and gave in to the peaceful pull of sleep. The battle between science and sleep might never end, but for now, sleep has won.

Chapter 5: The "New Dawn"

As the sun rose higher, filling the lab with warm shades of orange and yellow, the Night Owl Researchers could feel the weight of exhaustion pulling them down like a cozy blanket. One by one, they gave in, sinking into their chairs with eyes slowly closing, only to be interrupted by the sound of Ramesh, laughing loudly.

"You all look like you have been fighting the universe itself!" Ramesh joked, noticing their messy hair, which stuck out in all directions like they had just been through a storm.

"Or fighting our own sleep deprivation," Maya mumbled, rubbing her eyes as if trying to erase the tiredness.

They blinked at the bright sunlight streaming into the lab, slowly coming back to their senses. They exchanged looks, remembering the chaos of the night. They may not have uncovered the secrets of the universe, but they had certainly learned a lot about their own limits and the power of caffeine. All night, their experiments kept running, while their minds struggled to stay awake. "Okay, time to switch the FPLC sample again!" Vidya called out, trying to shake off the sleepiness as they kept going.

"Who knew that running experiments could feel so much like a night at the disco?" Rahul joked after one particularly chaotic hour, where they had accidentally mixed up their notes with aloo paratha orders. "I mean, look at these data points—they are practically doing the cha-cha!"

Vidya rolled her eyes but couldn't suppress her laughter. "Next thing you know, we will be analyzing the correlation between dance moves and enzyme activity. 'The Cha-Cha of Coffee Chemistry'—it could be a hit!"

Rahul pointed dramatically at a messy chart, "I can see it now! Each data point corresponds to a step in the dance. A little twist here, a shimmy there—voilà! We have unlocked the secrets of the universe, one groove at a time!"

"Just wait until our peer reviewers get a load of this," Maya chuckled, "They will be dancing right out of the lab with confusion!"

As their laughter faded, the trio exchanged confused looks, each secretly wondering if they had crossed into a world where too much caffeine made everything absurd. The chaos of their experiment felt like a weird dream, and the more they thought about it, the funnier it became. They could almost convince themselves that their exhausted minds had turned the lab into a strange mix of science and comedy.

Every time they turned around, it seemed like their sleep-deprived brains were playing tricks on them. At one point, Rahul was convinced that the spectrometer was talking back to him. "If I could just understand its language," he sighed, "I am sure it would give me the answers to all my life problems."

Amid all the chaos and laughter, they remained serious about their work. Each sample swap was important for their research, even if their eyelids felt like they weighed a ton. Despite the exhaustion, the energy in the lab stayed high, and the camaraderie between them was undeniable. They all knew they were in this together, and that sense of shared purpose was comforting.

Looking back on the night, they couldn't help but smile at the bond they had. They had not unlocked the secrets of the universe, but they had discovered something valuable: creativity often bloomed in the most unexpected hours. Sometimes, the best ideas came not from strict experiments but from those random, silly moments of brainstorming and laughter.

Finally, as they regained enough energy to talk about their experiments, Vidya half-jokingly said, "Well, we have definitely gathered enough data for a paper on the 'Effects of Sleep Deprivation on Research Productivity.' It could be groundbreaking, or at least ground-shaking!"

As they made plans for their next nocturnal adventure, Vidya raised her mug, holding the last of her magical coffee. "Here's to the Night Owl Researchers—may our caffeine always be strong and our ideas even stronger!"

Laughter filled the lab as they got ready for another night of fun discoveries. They were prepared to face the chaos of science and life because one thing they had learned was that a bit of tiredness often leads to a lot of creative ideas. After all, in the world of research, the line between genius and madness was often just a few cups of coffee away.

As they packed up and started talking about their upcoming experiments, Vidya grinned and said, "And remember friends, if you are ever in doubt whether to sleep or stay awake for science, just know: sleep is overrated, but coffee is a miracle. Just be careful not to mix up your data with your dinner orders, or you might end up with a 'Paneer Tikka Protein Analysis' instead!"

With that sage advice, the Night Owl Researchers were off again into the night, ready to uncover the mysteries of science, one caffeine-fueled adventure at a time.

Take Home—Embracing the spirit of research in India

As we navigate the ever-evolving landscape of research in India, we must recognize the incredible potential and responsibility that rests on our shoulders as researchers. In a country brimming with diverse cultures, rich biodiversity, and unique challenges, our work is not just a pursuit of knowledge; it is about making a real difference in the world around us. Here are some guiding thoughts to motivate you on your research journey.

Stick with It!

Research can feel like a never-ending roller coaster. There will be ups and downs, maybe a few loop-de-loops along the way, and long nights fueled by caffeine and creativity! However, it is this very perseverance that makes you a true researcher. Remember, every failed experiment is just a stepping stone to success. So, when things get tough, remind yourself: every "oops" is just part of the journey to a big "Eureka!"

Team Up!

In today's world, teamwork really does make the dream work. Partnering with other researchers, universities, or industries can supercharge your efforts and spark new ideas. In our country, with so many brilliant minds around, teamwork can lead to groundbreaking discoveries that could change lives. So, don't hesitate to share your wacky ideas and seek out collaborations—it might just lead to something fantastic!

Stay Curious!

Curiosity is the secret sauce of research! Always ask questions and look for new adventures. Whether you are working on improving farming techniques, developing new medicines, or solving environmental puzzles, your curiosity is the key to finding innovative solutions. After all, who knows what exciting discoveries are waiting just around the corner?

Mix It Up!

Today's challenges are like a spicy curry—best enjoyed with a mix of flavors! Don't limit yourself to a single discipline; draw from different fields to find fresh solutions. Such an interdisciplinary approach can help tackle problems from all angles and come up with ideas that are truly groundbreaking

Keep Learning!

The world of research is constantly changing, like the latest Bollywood blockbuster! New tools and ideas pop up all the time. Stay updated and be willing to learn, unlearn, and relearn. Engage in workshops, conferences, and online courses. It's all about keeping your skills sharp and your brain buzzing!

The Future of Research in India—Dancing Between Dreams and Discoveries

As students embark on their research adventure, remember that what you do truly matters! Your work has the potential to change lives, shape policies, and inspire the next generation of scientists. In today's rapidly changing world, scientists play a vital role in addressing challenges—from climate change to healthcare innovations. Your research can make a real difference. So, like our beloved Night Owl Researchers, let your dedication shine, your curiosity roam, and your impact grow. Embrace those late nights filled with caffeine and creativity, where every experiment, whether successful or not, is a lesson in disguise. Research is not just about getting it right the first time; it's about exploring, questioning, and daring to dream big. Each late-night brainstorming session can lead to groundbreaking ideas. The laughter shared among colleagues during chaotic experiments fuels your passion for discovery.

So, let's make Indian research a wild and wonderful ride together! Keep pushing boundaries, questioning the status quo, and celebrating every little victory. As you dance between dreams and discoveries, cherish the journey. Your efforts will inspire future generations to join this incredible adventure. This will pave the way for a brighter future in Indian research, where every step is a dance toward progress!

Disclaimer: *This story is completely made up, but it is inspired by the funny struggles of Indian researchers who are working late in the lab. If it sounds like your own lab with sleep-deprived scientists, well, that's purely a coincidence. It is all meant to be fun! If you feel upset, feel free to send your complaints through the nearest working lab equipment... if you can find one!*

7

When Lab Mice Go Rogue

It was just another Thursday morning at the Department of Biological Sciences, National Institute of Scientific Research (NISR). Professor Prakash Deshmukh had spent the entire two weeks getting ready for his next big experiment. He was not the type to leave things to chance. After years of dealing with the ups and downs of research, he had learned to plan everything carefully, double-check his work, and then check it again for good measure. This experiment, he was certain, would bring him closer to that major research grant he had been hoping for, one he had been eyeing for months like a hawk.

The experiment sounded simple enough—test a new supplement on lab mice to boost their memory and cognitive abilities. And not just any supplement, but a revolutionary one. The kind of thing that could make a researcher famous, get a shiny publication in a high-impact journal, and, of course, attract more funding than anyone could possibly require for lab supplies.

Professor Deshmukh had gathered all the necessary ingredients for success: a pristine, sterile lab, a fresh batch of genetically modified mice (the little test subjects were practically clones of each other, ready for their big moment), and a government grant of ₹50 lakhs. Now, to the newcomers, ₹50 lakh might sound like a lot of money, but anyone who has worked in Indian academia knows that in the world of biological research, this amount barely scratches the surface. It is enough to cover the basic costs of minor equipment, lab supplies, and maybe even a little extra for those surprise expenses that always seem to pop up. But still, for a researcher like Deshmukh, it was enough to spark a dream. A dream of groundbreaking research and, more importantly, a publication that would be the talk of NISR. This was his moment, and he was ready to grab it.

But little did Deshmukh know, his lab mice, those innocent little creatures he had always seen as just test subjects, had their own ideas. Ideas that would soon turn his perfectly planned experiment into a full-blown disaster. What happened next was so out of control, so unexpected, that even Deshmukh, despite all his years of reading research papers and planning experiments, could never have predicted it.

Chapter 1: The "Mice and Their Sudden Intelligence"

Professor Deshmukh, or "Prof. PD," as his students liked to call him, was always proud of how organized his lab was. Every experiment was planned down to the tiniest detail, with a level of precision that would make any bureaucrat jealous. He was the definition of discipline, something he had mastered after years of navigating the paperwork-heavy world of Indian academia and somehow getting his research proposals approved, almost by magic.

His lab was exactly what you would expect from any research facility at NISR—spotless, sterile, and serious. Everything was in its place. But on this particular day, something felt... off. As Deshmukh carefully injected his herbal supplement, made from some obscure local plant that was supposedly great for boosting brainpower, he noticed something strange. The mice, who had been calm and easy to manage for weeks, were now looking unusually... alert. In fact, they were too alert. Something was definitely not right.

It all started when one of the mice, who had been given the creative name Maximus by the research students (a name that clearly reflected the level of creativity in the lab), stood up on its hind legs and gave Professor Deshmukh a look that could only be described as a glare. At first, Deshmukh thought he was just seeing things, probably because he had not slept in two days. But then, something even stranger happened. The other mice started doing the same thing. They all stood up, one by one, and began staring at him with unblinking eyes.

"Okay, I definitely need more sleep," Deshmukh mumbled to himself, rubbing his eyes. But it wasn't just that the mice were standing. No, they seemed to be... communicating. Communicating! With each other. And maybe, just maybe, with him.

"I must be losing it," Deshmukh muttered, shaking his head and trying to focus on his notes, as though that would somehow help him ignore what was happening right in front of him.

But then, as he turned to write down the dosages for the next round of injections, he heard a soft rustling sound. He quickly turned around and saw Maximus and two other mice climbing up the side of the cage, as if it were a tiny, furry version of Mount Everest. The mice were not just trying to escape; they seemed to be on a mission. It looked like they were planning a full-on rebellion.

"Uh, Karan! Get in here!" Deshmukh screamed, his voice rising in panic. "We have a situation!"

Karan, a research student who cared more about getting his paper accepted than actually focusing on the research, rushed into the lab.

"What's happening, sir? What is the emergency?" Karan asked.

"I think the mice are planning something," Deshmukh said, pointing at the chaos unfolding in front of him. The mice were now using their tiny paws to unfasten their cages, like they had a set of mini tools and knew exactly how to break free.

Karan blinked in confusion. "But... sir, aren't they supposed to just... run in the maze and do things? Not form a union and overthrow us?"

"I think we are about to witness the first rodent revolution in scientific history," Deshmukh replied, already regretting every experimental decision that had led to this moment.

Chapter 2: The "Intensification of Revolution"

With the mice now freely roaming the lab, chaos quickly erupted. These mice were not just aimlessly running around like you would expect—no, they had a plan—a mission. One mouse in particular, who Deshmukh had jokingly named "Einstein" because of its unusually large ears, seemed to be taking charge. Einstein was clearly the brains of the operation. It did not waste time exploring the usual corners of the lab; instead, it headed straight for the computers.

Within minutes, Einstein had chewed through the power cables of Deshmukh's personal computer, causing the screen to flicker and then go completely black. The mouse just sat there, looking pleased with itself, as if it had just solved a major problem.

"Great, now I'll have to rewrite the entire proposal," Deshmukh muttered under his breath, staring at the dead computer screen. "Just what I needed today."

Meanwhile, Maximus, the original troublemaker, had found his way to the snack cupboard. There, he and his fellow escapees began feasting on leftover aloo paratha slices the students had carelessly tossed aside the night before. But it wasn't just food they were after. The mice had also discovered a stash of research papers, which they now appeared to be studying, as if mocking the entire PhD process. It was as if they were holding their own little conference, discussing the latest breakthroughs in butter consumption and cage escapes.

As the mice scattered in all directions, Deshmukh and Karan tried desperately to round them up. Karan, in his usual style of chaotic panic, grabbed a plastic container and attempted to trap one of the mice. But instead of catching anything, he knocked over a jar of formaldehyde, which rolled off the counter and spilled its contents across the floor. The fumes spread quickly, and both of them were immediately hit with a wave of strong, noxious air.

Deshmukh and Karan began coughing uncontrollably, barely able to catch their breath.

"This is exactly how not to run a research lab," Karan managed to say between coughs, his voice husky from the fumes.

Meanwhile, the mice seemed to be having the time of their lives. They were scaling shelves like tiny mountain climbers, dodging syringes like seasoned escape artists, and chewing through the research papers Deshmukh had spent the last six months carefully compiling. It was as if they had an inborn talent for ruining his career. One particularly adventurous mouse even managed to leap onto the high shelf where Deshmukh's prized microscope was sitting, and started examining it, as if it had some deep, scientific insight to offer.

"Well, that's just perfect," Deshmukh sighed, wiping the sweat from his forehead in disbelief. "A mouse with more interest in microscopy than I have ever had."

But the situation was only getting worse. Maximus, no longer content with just munching on scraps, had somehow figured out how to hack into the institute's email system. Now, he was sending out strange, cryptic messages to faculty members. Deshmukh received one such email with the subject line: "We Demand More Cheese!" It was followed by an outlandish request for "10% ownership of the lab equipment."

"I… I have no words," Deshmukh muttered, staring at the screen in utter disbelief. "This is either the end of my career or the beginning of something far more revolutionary than I ever could have imagined."

Chapter 3: The "Aftermath"

By the time the lab staff and a few other researchers managed to catch all the mice and get the lab back in order, Deshmukh realized that his experiment was completely ruined. The lab, once neat and clean, now looked like a disaster zone. There were overturned cages, papers scattered everywhere, and the smell of chaos in the air. Deshmukh stood in the middle of the mess, unsure whether to laugh or cry. But the mice? They were not upset at all. They had tasted freedom, and they liked it. They were not just test subjects anymore. They were little rebels who had experienced what it was like to escape, and they wanted more.

The institute did not know what to think about the whole thing, but it definitely became a great story for conferences. Researchers and students would joke about it in the hallways, asking Deshmukh, "How's the revolution going in your lab?" Some even joked about when the mice would start their next takeover. Deshmukh's lab had become the talk of the department, but not for any of the reasons he had planned.

As for the mice, they became famous on campus. They were now known as the clever little mice who started a rebellion in the lab. They were often mentioned by students and researchers, who now joked that maybe the mice were more intelligent than they were. The mice had become the symbol of a new group of researchers who were not afraid to question the way things were done.

And Professor Deshmukh? Well, he learned an important lesson from all this: when it comes to research, expect the unexpected. Things can go totally out of control, and sometimes your lab mice might just outsmart you and start their own research program. Deshmukh could only hope that, in the future, his mice would stick to running in mazes instead of starting revolutions.

In the weeks that followed, Deshmukh had to explain the whole situation to the funding agency. He had to send an email, and it was the most honest, and probably the most embarrassing email he had ever written. It said: "Dear Council of Basic Research, I regret to inform you that the lab mice in our experiment have developed an unexpected level of intelligence, to the point of attempting a takeover of the lab. Because of this, the experiment on cognitive enhancement has been... drastically changed. I apologize for the inconvenience this may cause." Deshmukh read over the email and could not believe how crazy it sounded, but there was no turning back now.

The reply came quickly: "Can you replicate this? It sounds more interesting than the original proposal."

Deshmukh stared at the screen in shock. The funding agency wanted him to recreate this? The mice were already plotting rebellions, and now the agency wanted him to bring them back for more? Deshmukh was not sure whether to laugh or cry at this point.

Take Home—Embracing uncertainty and adaptability in research

The story of Professor Deshmukh and his clever lab mice teaches us important lessons about research. Although the story is funny and full of unusual situations, it offers real insights for researchers.

Be ready for surprises

One key lesson is that science is often unpredictable. No matter how well you plan, unexpected things can happen. Professor Deshmukh's experiment, aimed at making mice smarter, took a wild turn when the mice became smarter than anyone expected. This shows that even carefully designed research can lead to surprising results. Scientists must stay flexible, ready to adapt, and open to unexpected outcomes.

In life science research, this unpredictability is especially common. Living organisms, whether animals or humans, do not always behave as expected. Experiments can be influenced by factors like genetics, environment, or even the mood of the subjects being studied. This uncertainty is part of the process, and researchers must stay alert and willing to adjust their plans when things change.

The importance of observation

The story also shows how important observation is in research. At first, Professor Deshmukh ignores the strange behavior of mice, thinking he is just tired. But when he looks closer, he realizes the mice are not just reacting, but they are actively planning to escape and create chaos. This teaches us that paying close attention is crucial in research. Following protocols and running experiments is not enough. Scientists must stay alert and notice what is really happening in the lab. Sometimes, unexpected discoveries come not from what we plan, but from what we observe when things go wrong. Think about the story of Alexander Fleming, who accidentally discovered antibiotics because he noticed something unusual. It shows that research often depends on being curious and paying close attention.

The role of communication

The story also highlights the value of communication. When Professor Deshmukh writes to the funding agency, he is honest about what happened. While the idea of rebelling mice seems funny, his honesty helps maintain trust and credibility. Clear communication is essential in research, whether it is with funding agencies, colleagues, or the public. It allows researchers to explain their work and findings, even when results are surprising or hard to understand.

Embracing the human side of research

The story also shows us the human side of research. People often think research is always serious and well-planned, but we must remember that scientists are human, too. In Professor Deshmukh's lab, there were mistakes, funny moments, and frustrations. Yet, it reminds us that humor, humility, and learning from failures are key parts of research. Research can be challenging, and things don't always go as planned, but those problems can lead to new ideas and discoveries.

The Future of Research in India—Keen Observation and Uncovering Opportunities

The story of Professor Deshmukh and his playful lab mice taught us valuable lessons about the future of research in India. It shows both the challenges our researchers face and the opportunities to improve and grow. The future of research in India depends on accepting change, solving problems, and working together. As researchers improve their skills, work with others, and focus on careful observation and clear communication, they can solve big problems and make important discoveries..

To make this happen, we need more support, better resources, and a fresh way of thinking about research. This is where the NEP 2020 comes in. NEP 2020 aims to create a better environment for research in India, making it easier for scientists to overcome challenges and achieve great things.

Disclaimer: *The story is purely fictional. Any resemblance to actual scientific experiments, lab mishaps, or rodent revolutions is purely a coincidence. No lab mice were harmed, recruited for a PhD program, or subjected to cognitive enhancement experiments. Any claims regarding mice plotting* *hostile takeovers are completely exaggerated and not endorsed by any ethical animal research protocols. Professor Deshmukh, though remarkably adaptable, is not responsible for any global scientific breakthroughs sparked by his lab's chaos. If you deal with intelligent rodents, be careful, and always be ready for surprises!*

8

The Paradox of Promotions in Academia

Sometimes, young faculty members feel like they are trapped in a pressure cooker. And no, it is not the kind of pressure you feel when you are worrying about a bad dinner or emotional crisis. No, this is the real deal—a pressure created by high academic expectations. The lid is tightly on, steam is rising, and there is no way out. What is the pressure? It is the never-ending, exhausting expectation that young researchers must publish or perish. There is no middle ground—publish, or you are done.

But here is the thing: we are not talking about the kind of publishing that results in the next great discovery in physics or medicine. Oh no. It is about meeting certain requirements. For many young academics, the publishing game is focussed on numbers, and not the actual content. It is like being told to run a marathon where no one cares if you finish first or last (just as long as you finish). The problem is the system that values quantity over quality creates a culture where creativity, original ideas, and the simple joy of doing research are pushed aside.

And here is where the promotion paradox comes in. It is not just about the papers you publish. To get promoted, you also have to complete a list of workshops and courses that are mandatory, even if they have nothing to do with your actual research. These courses end up being more important than the real contributions you make to your field.

Yes, you heard that right. You could publish groundbreaking research in high-quality journals, but if you haven't attended these courses, your promotion could still be held up. On the flip side, if you publish something with little value or originality in a barely-known journal, as long as you have checked off the required courses, you will move up the ladder. This creates a strange system where ticking formal requirements matters more than doing meaningful research. It rewards compliance over creativity and paperwork over progress.

But fear not, dear reader, this is not a hopeless tale. No, in fact, this story has a twist—and we are here to explore how we can untangle this academic mess, step by step, with a touch of optimism (because, honestly, without that, we would have all given up years ago).

Chapter 1: The "Publish or Perish Saga"

Let's get one thing straight: "publish or perish" is not just a catchy slogan in India—it is the way academia works. It is so deeply rooted in the system that every young faculty feels like it is a must-do to get ahead. The rules are simple: to move forward in your career, you need to publish a certain number of papers. The exact number changes depending on who you ask, but it is always the same idea. It doesn't matter if the papers are groundbreaking or if anyone even reads them. What matters is how many you have.

Now, imagine you are a young researcher in this environment. You have just started your career. Your lab isn't exactly brimming with resources, your funding isn't exactly stable, and your senior colleagues are, shall I say, not exactly helping you much. And yet, there you are, you keep submitting papers to journals that care more about fees than the quality of your research. You publish. You get a promotion. You publish more. You get more funding. Rinse and repeat. It's a cycle.

Does it matter that some of these journals are barely read or have no real impact? Not at all. As long as you publish, you are on the right track! It is all about filling your CV. More publications, more recognition. More… empty achievements.

But here is the problem: this system isn't just stressful; it is actually harmful. Instead of encouraging deep, meaningful research, it rewards speed over substance and quantity over quality. The result? A generation of faculties stuck on a treadmill, constantly churning out papers that don't really move research forward or solve real-world problems.

Chapter 2: The "Illusion of Meritocracy"

Now, let's talk about what happens when this pressure cooker heats up too much. The idea of "publish and advance" starts to fall apart. The illusion of meritocracy starts to crack. The belief that you can measure someone's worth by the number of papers they publish is a myth. But research doesn't really work that way, does it? Some of the greatest discoveries in the world didn't come from a steady stream of mediocre publications—they came from bold ideas, taking risks, and, importantly, time. Time to think. Time to experiment. Time to fail.

Many researchers now keep churning out papers as if they are the next big thing (when they are really not). The pressure on young faculties is so high that they start to wonder if it is even worth exploring bold ideas that might take years to develop. It is much easier to take a safe approach, quickly put together a paper, and send it off to a journal that promises fast publication. It doesn't matter if the research is not groundbreaking, as long as it gets published, right?

The real problem is that this constant pressure to publish often leads to a kind of academic burnout. Instead of being motivated by curiosity and the desire to solve real-world problems, young researchers end up exhausted, disappointed, and trapped in the cycle of publishing more and more papers. They are so focused on meeting publication demands that they don't have the time or mental energy to think about innovative ideas or take on more complex research that could actually make a difference.

Chapter 3: The "System That is Supposed to Reward Innovation"

Let's pause here and look at the irony of it all. Academia, at its best, is supposed to be a space for innovation—where faculties can challenge the norm, explore the unknown, and create knowledge that pushes boundaries. And yet, what are young researchers being told? "Publish! Publish! And do it fast!" Forget original ideas, forget research that could take years to solve global problems—what matters is the list of papers you can put on your CV.

It is as though the research system is treating young faculties like vending machines: put in some data, press a button, and voilà! Out comes another paper. The less you think about it, the better. After all, it's all about quantity that counts. As long as you keep producing, you are on the right track. Never mind the lack of groundbreaking discoveries or the fact that your papers may never be read again. The system wants you to repeat the same thing over and over, just in slightly different ways. It is a recipe for mediocrity, not innovation.

Chapter 4: The "Promotion Paradox"

Ah, promotions—the big dream for every faculty member. You have spent years working hard, publishing papers, and maybe even getting your research into some prestigious journals. You have contributed to your field and advanced knowledge, right? Well, not so fast. Before you can climb that promotion ladder, there is one more hurdle: faculty development programs, refresher courses, orientation courses, and the like. Because apparently, groundbreaking research is not enough. What really matters is ticking boxes.

It doesn't matter if your research could transform your field or benefit society. If you have not attended the required courses, forget about that promotion. And what do these courses teach? Oh, essentials like "How to Use MS Word Like a Pro" or "Time Management for People Too Busy to Manage Their Time." Groundbreaking research methodologies? Nope. Becoming a thought leader in your field? Not a priority. The real skill in Indian academia? Checking off boxes on your course completion certificates.

Now, let's flip the script. Suppose you dutifully attend all these sessions, sit through hours of redundant slideshows, and collect participation certificates. Congratulations! As long as you have completed the courses, it doesn't matter what you have published. Got your name on a paper in a journal that no one has ever heard of? A paper that contributes absolutely nothing meaningful? No problem—promotion is almost guaranteed.

So, to sum it up, You could publish innovative, high-impact research in prestigious global journals, but if you skipped that mandatory two-week refresher course on "Effective Time-Saving Techniques," you are stuck. Meanwhile, someone else who spent their time attending every single course, while publishing mediocre papers in obscure journals, is cruising up the promotion ladder. The message is clear: completing mandatory courses is more valuable than actual academic brilliance.

This system values compliance over creativity and meaningful research; it rewards ticking administrative boxes. Promotions are not based on advancing knowledge or solving real-world problems, they are based on proving you have jumped through all the right hoops. And just for good measure, you will be applauded for "adapting to the evolving demands of academia," as if knowing how to write a proper email is the height of scholarly achievement.

Isn't academia just wonderful?

Chapter 5: The "Story of Riya"

Let's talk about Riya, a passionate young scientist fresh out of her PhD from the Indian Institute of Transformative Research. She was brimming with dreams—dreams of groundbreaking research, solving real-world problems, and making a difference through research. Publishing papers was not her goal; it was a means to explore new research areas and share meaningful discoveries with the world.

But reality had other plans. In her first year as a faculty member at the university, Riya faced an unrelenting wave of deadlines and constant pressure from her peers to "publish or perish." Her lab, which she hoped would be a hub of innovation, turned out to be little more than a glorified storage space—barely equipped for basic experiments, let alone cutting-edge research. The message was loud and clear: her career was not going anywhere unless she produced at least three publications in her first two years.

At first, Riya thought she could manage it. She planned to balance her experiments and write papers on the side, believing research was about quality, not just quantity. But the truth hit hard. In the academic world, she found herself in, it was not about producing meaningful work—it was all about numbers. The research itself? That could wait. Experiment failure? No problem, as long as there was something to publish. Original ideas? Too risky. The clock was ticking, and safe, quick-to-complete studies were her only way to meet the paper quota.

By the end of the second year, Riya had three publications. But none of them were truly groundbreaking.

They were small, unremarkable studies, quick and safe but far from her lofty dreams of making a real impact. Worse, she was exhausted, disillusioned, and felt like she was simply cranking out papers to keep her job. Research had been replaced with a never-ending production line of mediocrity.

And just when Riya thought things couldn't get worse, she discovered another strange paradox: promotions didn't just depend on publishing papers. To climb the career ladder, she had to complete mandatory courses. Yes, you read that right. Even publications would not guarantee promotion if she had not attended courses and programs on, say, "Time Management for Overworked Academics" or "Basics of Research Methodology." Did these courses help with research or innovation? Not at all. Yet, they were mandatory. The ultimate irony? Publishing in prestigious, high-quality journals would not secure her promotion without those certificates. But completing the courses and publishing in unknown, low-quality journals? Promotion is practically guaranteed.

It was absurd. The system that was supposed to reward real research, creativity, and long-term scientific advancement rewarded compliance and box-ticking. It didn't matter if her work advanced research or solved critical problems. As long as she had the certificates and the right number of papers, the promotion would follow, even if those papers were mediocre at best.

Riya understood the problem but felt helpless to change it. She was stuck in a system that cared more about rules and numbers than real talent or meaningful work.

She didn't just want promotions or fancy titles; all she wanted was to do real, important research. But the system gave her no choice.

To stay afloat in her career, she had to keep publishing papers, no matter how pointless, and attend endless courses. The more she tried to focus on solving real problems, the more the system dragged her into this endless cycle. Without the certificates and low-quality publications, her career would stop. But with them, she had no time or freedom to do real research.

Over time, Riya's passion for meaningful work started to fade. She stopped dreaming about making a difference and focused only on surviving the maze. A brilliant scientist with so much potential was lost in a system that cared more about ticking boxes than creating real change.

Chapter 6: How to fix this "Without Losing Our Minds?"

Now that we have all taken a moment to realize just how the system is, let us focus on finding some real solutions. I am not saying these fixes will be easy, but they are necessary if we want meaningful research to come out of our universities instead of more of the same boring, quantity-driven papers. So, let's think outside the box (yes, I know it's risky, but let's give it a try.)

Rethink metrics for success

First things first: it is high time we stop thinking that success in academia is only about the number of papers you publish. Seriously, when did academia become a glorified paper factory? Instead, we need a system that rewards research for its originality, depth, and impact. Did your research address a major global issue? Could it help solve real-world problems or improve lives? Did it provide a deeper understanding of a fundamental phenomenon?

That, my friends, is the kind of research we should be celebrating—not just the one with the trending topics or the short-term attention. It is about time we recognize that real innovation does not always come from pumping out paper after paper.

Make space for innovation

Let's be honest: this obsession with churning out paper after paper is suffocating creativity. Young faculty members are so busy meeting submission deadlines and increasing publication numbers that they hardly have time to think big. To truly push the boundaries of research, they need the space to fail, experiment, and explore new ideas without constantly worrying about meeting publication targets. Long-term, high-risk research opportunities projects that might not yield immediate results but could lead to major discoveries are the way forward. Some of the most exciting scientific ideas are the hardest to execute and do not fit into a neat three-year-end project completion report.

Focus on quality research

Let's touch on something that is essential to fixing this problem: the promotion paradox. We have all seen it in action. Take Riya, for instance. She could have published groundbreaking papers in top journals, but if she has not completed the mandatory courses, she would not get promoted. It is no longer about the quality of her research; it is about ticking off boxes for courses that have little to no relevance to do with her actual research skills. She could produce work as impactful as Einstein's, but if she has not attended the required courses, her promotion is at risk.

The system ties career growth to administrative checklists rather than the actual value of the contributions. The good news? This can change. Promotions should be based on the value someone adds to their field. We need to start recognizing the real impact a faculty member's work has on the world. It's time to fix the system before young faculty lose their minds. We need to change how we measure success, encourage new ideas, and guide the next generation of faculty. Otherwise, talented researchers will stay stuck in a cycle of pointless numbers and courses. Riya's story (and many others) shows that we still have a long way to go, but with the right changes, we can create a place where quality and creativity really matter.

Take Away—Time to change the system

The pressure to publish in Indian academia is real, and yes, it is making young faculty struggle. But here is the good news: it can be changed. The focus can shift from a system that values the number of papers to one that values their quality and impact. An environment can be created where young researchers are encouraged to take risks, explore new ideas, and make real contributions to research, instead of simply checking off boxes for promotions.

However, it is not just the pressure to publish that needs reform. The promotion paradox in academia is just as damaging. It is high time we stop rewarding faculty members just for completing courses that have little to do with their actual research. The focus should shift to their contributions to their field, the originality of their work, and the positive societal impact it can create.

This change would not happen overnight, but with the right reforms, young faculty can escape the pressure cooker. They can produce the kind of work that matters, not just for their promotions but for the future of research. The kind of work that not only fills academic journals but actually makes a difference in addressing global challenges.

While the book was in press, the UGC released a draft of the "UGC Regulations on Minimum Qualifications for Appointment of Teachers and Other Academic Staff in Universities and Colleges and Measures for the Maintenance of Standards in Higher Education." This is a crucial and significant step, and let's hope it will address critical issues, including not only the qualifications for appointment but also the promotion process.

So, let's get to work, shall we? Because if we don't change how we measure academic success and promotions, the next generation of researchers will continue to be stuck like Riya, with no way out. And that would be a true academic tragedy.

The Future of Research in India—A Shift Toward Impact and Innovation

To unlock the full potential of our researchers, we need a fundamental shift in how academic success is evaluated. The current obsession with quantity over quality must give way to a system that values meaningful, impactful research. Success should not be about churning out papers but about conducting research that addresses real-world problems and advances knowledge in significant ways.

Indian researchers have the talent to make a real impact, but they need the freedom to explore new ideas without the constant pressure of meeting publishing targets. The promotion system, too, requires an overhaul. Young scientists should be allowed to think creatively, take risks, and push the boundaries of knowledge. If we focus on quality, creativity, and real-world impact, the future will be bright. An academic system that values meaningful work and supports young researchers in solving real problems will not only strengthen our scientific community but also help us to address the pressing challenges. The time to make these changes is now.

Disclaimer: *The narrative you have just read is a mix of reality, frustration, and a dash of optimism. While the scenarios may sound familiar to many, they are meant to highlight the challenges faced by young faculties in India. Any resemblance to actual persons, living or dead, is purely coincidental—unless, of course, you are an overworked researcher in academia, in which case, you might want to take a deep breath and keep reading for some hope!*

9

The Mentorship Gap

In the fast-paced and ever-changing world of academic research, faculty members are often expected to wear many hats. They are not just researchers; they are also teachers, administrators, and, quite frequently, unofficial counselors for stressed-out students. (let's be honest; the number of times a student says, "Can I talk to you about something personal?" is enough to make you wonder if you are running a therapy clinic on the side). With so many roles to manage, the need for good mentorship is very more important. Young faculties often find themselves lost in this maze of responsibilities without anyone to guide them. They are left to figure out everything on their own, from setting up labs to decoding the complicated rules of the functioning of the university system. It is like being handed a giant puzzle with no picture on the box and no one to tell you if the pieces even fit.

And here is the harsh truth: the mentorship gap is very real, and it has been quietly growing. Senior faculty, swamped with their own teaching, research, and meetings, often do not have the time (or at least say they don't) to mentor young faculties. As a result, these bright, eager minds are left to fend for themselves, stumbling through the chaotic maze of academia without the guidance they desperately need. This is not just a minor inconvenience; it is a serious problem that could slow down the growth of the next generation of faculties. Without proper mentorship, young academics might feel like they are trying to swim in a pool full of sharks (only to realize they are also allergic to water).

So, what can senior faculty and experienced scientists do to fill this mentorship gap? How can they step in and help their younger colleagues find their way in the complicated world of academia, where running a lab, dealing with administration, teaching classes, and keeping up with research all seem to demand 25 hours in a day? The solution is surprisingly simple: they need to share their experiences, offer practical guidance, and, most importantly, stop treating mentorship like a chore. (Because, let's face it, nobody has time for yet another full-time job.)

Senior faculty can make mentorship easier and more helpful by giving practical advice and sharing lessons they have learned over the years. Let us explore how they can help young faculties not just survive but thrive, without turning the whole experience into the academic version of a soap opera.

Chapter 1: The "I'm Too Busy" excuse

If you are a young faculty in India, there is a good chance that you have heard the infamous words: "I'm too busy. I don't have time to mentor you." And if you have heard it so often that you have considered forming a "Mentorship Abandoned" club, well, you are not alone. But before we dive into a dramatic rant about academic neglect, let's pause for a moment to understand the reality behind the "I'm too busy" excuse.

Senior faculty members are not exactly lounging around sipping chai and flipping through academic journals all day (as nice as that might sound). Their days are packed with responsibilities—endless meetings that somehow feel longer than their classes, publishing papers, guiding students, teaching courses, and trying to stay sane through it all. Oh, and let's not forget the administrative tasks, which somehow keep growing no matter how much they try to simplify them.

So, when mentoring gets added to this already impossible to-do list, it is like asking them to climb Mount Everest while carrying a backpack full of bricks. It is not that they do not want to help; it's that the thought of taking on even one more task can feel like the last straw.

But here's the thing: mentoring doesn't have to be some big, time-consuming task that requires weekly heart-to-heart sessions where you pour out all your academic wisdom like a guru on a mountaintop. It doesn't need to be a formal "let's have a meeting and make a plan" kind of thing either. Mentoring can be as simple as a quick chat over lunch, a few words of advice after class, or even a casual email with a helpful tip. It is not about being a full-time life coach; it is about showing young faculties that they are not navigating this messy academic journey all by themselves.

So, senior faculty, relax. Nobody is asking you to become a 24/7 mentor who is always on call, dishing out advice like a hotline. But when a young faculty looks lost or overwhelmed, you can step in with a few words of encouragement or share a trick or two to help them survive the chaos of academia. Sometimes, a small piece of advice can make a huge difference.

And let's be real—these young faculties are already doing their best to keep their lab running while battling the nightmare of paperwork that seems designed to test their patience. The least you can do is throw them a lifeline every now and then. Trust me; they will thank you for it. And who knows? Maybe they will even stop secretly calling you "too busy to care" behind your back.

Chapter 2: The "Power of Shared Experience"

One of the greatest treasures a senior faculty has (aside from their large list of published papers and a drawer full of conference badges) is the treasure chest of experience they have gained by surviving (and occasionally thriving) in the wilds of academia. From the whirlwind of setting up a lab to the mind-bending maze of administrative tasks, senior faculties have pretty much seen it all. Think of them as the battle-hardened generals of academia, except, instead of shiny medals, they carry a cupboard full of colorful coffee mugs from conferences and the unmistakable "I haven't slept in three days" look. But how can they pass on this hard-earned wisdom to their younger colleagues? Easy: by sharing it.

Let's take setting up a lab as an example (the ultimate rite of passage for a young faculty). It is the task nobody warns you about and no textbook covers. For them, setting up a lab feels a lot like being handed a box of random tools and told, "Build a rocket." Where do you even start? What equipment is essential? How do you write a funding proposal that doesn't land in the rejection pile? And which supplier should you trust—because, spoiler alert, the ones offering "unbeatable deals" might leave you with pipettes that break after three uses.

This is where a senior mentor can make all the difference. They have been through this process before (probably more times than they would like to admit) and can offer advice that goes way beyond the obvious. Sure, knowing where to buy the cheapest pipettes is handy (because who doesn't like saving money?), but the real value lies in the lessons they learned the hard way. Like how not to blow half your grant on shiny equipment you will use only once or how to navigate the process of writing funding proposals without completely losing your mind. It is about helping young faculties avoid the pitfalls that senior faculties learned to dodge after years of stumbling into them.

For example, a simple conversation about managing lab resources—like how to make sure you are not running out of essential supplies in the middle of an experiment (because who enjoys realizing they are out of reagents on a Friday night?), or how to keep track of lab inventory without turning it into a full-time job—can save months of frustration. It is these little tips, often learned the hard way (because, let's face it, everyone buys too many lab supplies in the beginning), that can prevent the kind of administrative headaches and budgetary nightmares that make you wonder if you have accidentally joined a reality TV show called "Lab Wars: Budgeting Gone Wrong."

So, senior mentors, the next time a younger faculty looks at you with wide eyes and asks for guidance, don't just hit them with the classic "figure it out" line. Instead, share your stories, your lessons, and, yes, your mistakes. Because those small bits of wisdom you pass along could save them from months of frustration, paperwork, and, most importantly, unnecessary stress. Academia is challenging enough as it is; they definitely don't need to reinvent the wheel. You have already survived the rollercoaster ride, so why not throw them a map and let them enjoy the ride with a little less screaming?

Chapter 3: The "Navigation through Administrative Mazes"

The academic system in India is practically an art form, and the bureaucracy feels like a never-ending maze. From government regulations to university rules that seem to be written in a language only bureaucrats understand, young faculties often find themselves buried in forms. It's like being given a treasure map with no "X" and no clue what you are actually searching for. This is where mentorship becomes more than just helpful; it is absolutely essential. Without guidance, young faculties are left struggling through a sea of forms, permissions, and rules, hoping they will somehow find the right way (Spoiler alert: they won't.)

Now, I know what you are thinking—admin work is not as exciting as running experiments or writing papers. But here is the truth: understanding and handling administrative tasks is a key part of running a successful lab. Think of it like the behind-the-scenes engine that keeps the research train moving. Without it, the train would just sit there, stuck in the station, surrounded by piles of paperwork and the dreaded "pending approval" stamp.

This is where senior faculty members come in. They have already survived this and can share their hard-earned knowledge with young faculties. Their guidance can help make the whole admin process less confusing and save time for what really matters: research. Here is how mentors can help guide young faculties through the paperwork mess:

Understanding grants and funding procedures: Applying for grants can feel like a game of "Who Knows What They're Doing?"—except instead of winning money, you risk losing your mind. Senior faculty can explain how to apply for grants correctly, what funding agencies really want (hint: they don't just want fancy words), and how to avoid the common mistakes that make your proposal look like it was written during a coffee break.

Hiring and managing lab personnel: Hiring the right research assistants or lab technicians is never easy. Senior mentors can give advice on how to choose the right team (and avoid hiring your friend's cousin who has no clue what a pipette is). They can also help with managing the team, which is almost as tricky as managing the entire lab inventory.

Compliance and ethics: Keeping research ethical is important (unless, of course, you are planning to create a mutant army of lab mice). Senior faculty can guide young faculties on the importance of following ethical guidelines and how to make sure their research meets university rules.

Think of them like a GPS—they will help you avoid going down the wrong path and ending up in a place called "What Did I Just Do?!"

When senior mentors share their knowledge of administrative processes, they are not just giving good advice—they are saving young faculties valuable time. Time that could be spent running experiments, writing papers, or even doing something fun (yes, that's still a thing). Because let us face it, no one wakes up thinking, "Today is the day I'm going to fill out 50 forms and get no research done." So, by guiding young faculties through these often-overlooked areas, mentors can make sure they spend less time buried in paperwork and more time doing what they love: research.

Chapter 4: The "Balance of Learning"

In the Indian university system, teaching and research are often treated like distant cousins who don't really get along. Yet, young faculty members are expected to do both really well. On top of that, they are given loads of administrative work too. Balancing all this can leave even the most hardworking faculties feeling overwhelmed.

This is where mentorship becomes really important. Senior faculty, who have years of experience managing these tasks, can guide young faculty to avoid burning out (literally and metaphorically). They can help you balance teaching, research, and administration before you end up crying over a mountain of paperwork in your office. Here is how senior mentors can help:

Manage time: No, you can't do everything at once (and no, you can't clone yourself—yet). Senior mentors can teach young faculty how to plan their day better, so they are not stuck grading papers when they should be writing a grant proposal or working on their research. The key is simple: plan ahead, and don't pretend you can handle everything at once. Trust me, no one expects you to be a superhero.

Delegate tasks: This is where young faculty often trip up. Young faculty often think they have to do everything themselves and still answer emails about the department picnic. Senior faculty can remind them that they don't need to be a one-person show. Delegating tasks like managing the lab can take a huge weight off their shoulders and give them more time to focus on what matters most—teaching, research, or maybe even just enjoying a quiet coffee.

Chapter 5: The "Personal and Professional Growth"

Mentorship is not just about teaching young faculties how to take classes, run experiments, or write papers; it is also about helping them grow personally and professionally. Senior faculty members, with their years of wisdom (and probably a few battle scars), can be role models, showing young faculties how to build a fulfilling career without completely losing their sanity. This is especially important in academia, where expectations can feel so overwhelming that even coffee breaks seem like a distant dream.

Senior faculties can also offer invaluable advice on handling rejection (because, let's be honest, rejection emails are like badges of honor in the research world). They can teach young faculties how to navigate the tricky academic landscape without losing their sense of self. Whether it is dealing with setbacks, managing stress, or realizing that success is not just about completing syllabus and publishing papers, mentors help young faculty members see the bigger picture. It's about making meaningful contributions to your field and, most importantly, staying true to the passion that inspired the teaching and research in the first place. Because if you lose that spark, all you will have left is a mountain of stress. And trust me, nobody wants that.

Chapter 6: The "Ripple Effect"

Mentorship often starts with one-on-one relationships between mentors and mentees, but the real goal should be to build a culture of mentorship across the entire institution. When senior faculty members take the time to engage with young faculties, they set a positive example that inspires the next generation of academics. After gaining some experience and hopefully a bit of wisdom, these mentees are more likely to become mentors themselves. And just like that, a beautiful cycle of knowledge sharing and collaboration begins (kind of like a slow-moving ripple in a calm pond, but way more useful than that metaphor sounds).

In Indian universities, where individual achievements often get more attention than teamwork, this shift in mindset is crucial. Mentorship should not be seen as just one person helping another; it should be a collaborative effort that benefits everyone. After all, if everyone focuses only on their own success, we end up with stressed-out faculties hoarding knowledge like it is the last slice of pizza at a party. But, when mentorship becomes a priority, it creates a supportive academic environment where young faculty members gain the skills and confidence they need to succeed, and the institution benefits from increased collaboration and innovation. So, let's make mentorship the new trend because when everyone wins, it is not just a good idea; it is a game changer.

Take Home-One mentor at a time

At the end of the day, bridging the mentorship gap is something that can be done with a bit of time, effort, and a lot of goodwill. Senior faculty members hold the experience, knowledge, and insight that can help young faculty members not just survive, but thrive in academia.

The main idea here is simple: mentorship is not just a favor; it is something institutions should value. When knowledge flows easily between generations, it builds innovation, teamwork, and strength. This kind of support ensures young faculty members do not feel lost but are encouraged to grow in an environment of respect and cooperation.

So, senior faculty, let us drop the "I'm too busy" excuse, roll up our sleeves, and invest in the next generation. And young faculties, don't hesitate to reach out. The guidance you need could be just a conversation away. After all, mentorship is not about handing over all the answers; it is about offering a little direction, encouragement, and maybe a few laughs along the way.

The Future of Research in India-Creating Bridges Through Mentorship

The future of research in India is full of possibilities, but achieving it will take more than just high-tech labs and big policies. It needs strong mentorship and teamwork. While we aim for great discoveries and higher global rankings, we must remember that young faculties are at the heart of this dream. They need more than technical skills; they need guidance and support to handle the challenges of academia. Experienced faculties, with their years of ups and downs, have a key role to play.

The key is to approach mentorship with a positive mindset. It does not have to be an enormous task. Sometimes, it is the small gestures—a word of advice, a word of encouragement, or a lesson learned the hard way—that make all the difference. So, if we want the future of research in India to shine brightly, we need to light the way for those who will carry the torch forward.

Our success in research depends on this teamwork to overcome challenges and create breakthroughs that inspire the world. The NEP 2020 is a roadmap, but its success depends on people—on mentors sharing wisdom and mentees embracing the journey. Let us build this future, step by step, one mentor at a time.

Disclaimer: *The advice offered here is a result of years of own experience, some hard lessons, and occasional moments of panic. While mentorship can definitely help, it is not* *a miracle fix for every academic challenge. No amount of guidance can guarantee instant success. Proceed with caution, and remember, even the best mentors can't help you if you forget to water your plants (or your teaching and research activities).*

10

The Path Forward: Building a Positive Research Mindset in Indian Academia

In a country as diverse and large as India, research has the power to solve unique problems and bring about significant changes. India has a strong history of intellectual achievements, with its knowledge system deeply rooted in ancient traditions. India has made important contributions in areas like mathematics, astronomy, medicine, philosophy, and languages. The Indian way of thinking has always encouraged new ideas and combining knowledge from different fields. Ancient texts like the *Vedas, Upanishads, Charaka Samhita, Aryabhatiya,* etc., show how research, science, spirituality, and practical use of knowledge (Bhāratīya Jñāna Paramparā) were closely connected. However, this valuable heritage is often not linked to modern teaching and research practices. India's research system is performing less well as compared to developed countries. India still faces challenges in areas like quality of research, global rankings, and innovation. This raises questions about its effectiveness, results, and long-term goals. These problems come from deeper issues that require a change in how research and development (R&D) activities are planned and conducted in Indian universities.

While the challenges are significant, they are not impossible to overcome. With the right mindset and practical strategies, India can transform and become a global leader in innovation and discovery. Let us discuss a few ideas that can help us drive this transformation and create a more dynamic and competitive research ecosystem.

1. Role of leadership and vision

Strong leadership is crucial for creating an environment that supports and values research. Leaders like vice-chancellors and directors are mainly responsible for shaping a culture that prioritizes intellectual freedom, collaboration, and the long-term vision of the institute. They must ensure that researchers have the freedom to explore new ideas, collaborate across different fields, and focus on finding innovative solutions to complex problems.

One of the most critical responsibilities of these leaders is to set clear and transparent research priorities aligned with regional, national, and global needs. By doing so, they guide universities and institutions toward impactful, meaningful work that can drive progress. Encouraging a focus on areas with potential for major breakthroughs in science, technology, and societal well-being is vital for creating a dynamic research culture.

At the same time, policymakers need to understand that research is a long-term commitment. It's not always about getting quick results or immediate returns. Some fields, like healthcare, renewable energy, and climate change, need many years, even decades, to show results. For example, a 10-year research project may not give immediate answers, but in the long run, it can make a big difference, like finding solutions to reduce dependence on fossil fuels or fighting climate change.

Therefore, both university leaders and policymakers should see research as a long-term investment. They need to create an environment where researchers can take on big projects that may not show results right away, but have the potential to lead to important discoveries. Having this long-term view is essential to building a strong and innovative research system in the future.

2. Encouraging quality over quantity

In India, there is a strong focus on the "publish or perish" culture. This focus on quantity often leads to researchers publishing in low-impact journals just to meet requirements for promotions or funding. As a result, the emphasis on publishing numbers comes at the cost of originality and critical thinking. This environment discourages researchers from focusing on truly innovative or groundbreaking work.

The actual focus should be on the quality and impact of research. Original work that tackles real-world problems, provides social value, and earns global recognition deserves greater appreciation. Innovative, high-impact research addressing key national challenges holds significant importance. Publications in reputable journals and research contributing meaningfully to society should naturally carry more weight. This shift in perspective will encourage impactful studies over mere quantity.

3. Promoting a culture of curiosity and risk-taking

Faculty members often hesitate to explore bold or unconventional ideas due to a fear of failure. To change this, an environment that encourages curiosity, creativity, and risk-taking, should be promoted. Providing seed funding for risky or uncertain ideas can inspire innovative thinking. Supporting faculty in experimenting freely can promote a culture of discovery that leads to breakthroughs and exciting new possibilities.

4. Increasing funding and infrastructure

India spends less than 1% of its GDP on R&D, which is much less than countries like the USA, China, Israel, and South Korea. To improve research, India should aim to spend at least 2% of its GDP, similar to global leaders. The government can also introduce policies to encourage private companies to invest in research by offering tax benefits or other rewards. If industries collaborate more closely with universities by sharing resources and funding research together, it can lead to better facilities and provide strong support for new ideas and innovations.

5. Reducing administrative burdens

Creating an environment where research is given equal importance as teaching is essential. Simplifying bureaucratic processes can also significantly help faculty focus on their core work. One way to do this is hiring skilled

The
Path
Forward

administrative staff to handle project-related paperwork and administrative tasks. This would free up faculties to devote more time to their studies and experiments.

6. Building a strong mentorship culture

Mentorship is key to the growth of young researchers. Senior faculty members should take an active role in guiding early-career faculties through the challenges of working in the university system. Both national and international platforms should be used to create more mentorship opportunities and connect young researchers with experienced mentors. This support can help them navigate their careers and reach their full potential.

7. Promoting collaboration and interdisciplinary research

Many of the world's biggest breakthroughs happen when ideas from different fields come together. Creating interdisciplinary research centers, where experts from various subjects collaborate, can make this easier. Specialized grants should prioritize projects that involve multiple disciplines. For example, tackling complex issues like climate change needs input from environmental science, economics, sociology, and engineering. Encouraging these kinds of collaborations can lead to smarter, more innovative solutions.

8. Strengthening industry-academia linkages

In many advanced countries, universities and industries work closely to solve practical problems. In India, this relationship needs to be improved. Universities collaborating with industries on research projects that address practical issues should be encouraged. Creating industrial advisory boards, joint PhD programs, and research fellowships funded by private companies can help get more industries involved in research. These partnerships can make sure that academic research leads to real-world solutions and has a lasting, meaningful impact.

9. Integrating traditional knowledge with modern research

Today, while there has been a steady increase in the number of universities, institutes, and research publications, the system still faces challenges in connecting its traditional knowledge with modern research. Integrating Bhāratīya Jñāna Paramparā with contemporary science offers a unique opportunity to harness the best of both worlds. For example, our rich heritage in traditional medicine, like Ayurveda and Siddha, has great potential for healthcare and drug discovery. Similarly, ancient knowledge about environmental science and sustainable living can offer solutions to modern problems like climate change. Unfortunately, these valuable areas are often overlooked in mainstream research and education.

To make the most of this knowledge, we need to combine traditional wisdom with modern teaching and research methods. Special centers to study ancient knowledge alongside modern subjects could be established. These centers can focus on translating ancient texts, scientifically testing traditional practices, and applying them to address current issues. This approach can blend the wisdom of the past with the advancements of the present to find innovative solutions.

With the introduction of NEP 2020, there have been efforts to document and preserve India's knowledge, such as digitizing old manuscripts and studying traditional practices. However, to make a real difference, these efforts need to be more closely connected to mainstream R&D. Combining ancient wisdom with modern technology can create new ideas that are not only competitive globally but also uniquely Indian.

Conclusion-Towards a Brighter Future for Indian Academia

India's research ecosystem holds vast potential that can drive progress and innovation on a global scale. However, to fully realize this potential, the mindset of researchers, administrators, and policymakers must shift to help create a research environment where groundbreaking ideas are nurtured, collaboration is encouraged, and solutions are developed for the challenges that affect both India and the world.

The time is ripe for India to embrace a research philosophy that is rooted in curiosity, resilience, and a collective vision for a better, more sustainable future. India's wealth of human resources, intellectual capital, and cultural diversity are unique strengths that can enable the country to take the lead in global scientific discovery. With the proper focus and alignment of efforts, we can not only contribute to global advancements but also offer solutions that are uniquely suited to the needs of our own diverse population.

As the world faces problems like climate change, healthcare challenges, and technological innovation, India has a critical role to play in finding answers. Our rich knowledge, talent, and resources should be channeled into research that tackles these global issues. Strengthening the research ecosystem through interdisciplinary collaboration and long-term vision will not only elevate India's status in the international scientific community but will also improve the lives of its people.

The path ahead requires commitment, but with the right mindset and a clear vision, India has the resources and potential to lead the world in scientific discovery and contribute significantly to solving global challenges. It is time to make this transformation happen for the benefit of future generations.

This transformation is not just a possibility; it is essential for realizing the vision of ViksitBharat@2047.

About the Author

Prof. Timir Tripathi (*b. 1981*) is a distinguished academic and molecular biologist, currently serving as a Professor in the Department of Zoology, School of Life Sciences, at North-Eastern Hill University, Shillong. His illustrious career has included roles such as Regional Director at Indira Gandhi National Open University, Kohima, Nagaland (2022–2023), and Senior Assistant Professor in the Department of Biochemistry at NEHU (2009–2022). Prof. Tripathi earned his Ph.D. from Jawaharlal Nehru University, New Delhi, while working at the Central Drug Research Institute, Lucknow. He has also served as a visiting faculty at Utkal University (Bhubaneswar), ICGEB (New Delhi), and Khon Kaen University (Thailand).

With a keen interest in understanding the mysteries of protein structure, function, and folding, his work extends into structure-based drug discovery. Prof. Tripathi is a recipient of several prestigious awards, including the NASI-Prof. B.K. Bachhawat Memorial Young Scientist Lecture Award (2020), ISCB-Young Scientist Award (2019), ICMR-Shakuntala Amir Chand Prize (2018), and BRSI-Malviya Memorial Award (2017), among others. He is an Associate Fellow of the Indian National Science Academy (INSA), New Delhi, and a member of the National Academy of Sciences, India (Prayagraj), as well as the Royal Society of Chemistry and Royal Society of Biology (UK).

A prolific contributor to scientific literature, Prof. Tripathi has over 150 publications to his name, including original research articles, reviews, and editorials in reputed international journals. His editorial contributions include editing six books and authoring two widely acclaimed textbooks for undergraduate and postgraduate students. He holds key editorial positions, including Senior Editor for Critical Insights in Biophysics (Taylor & Francis), Editor of International Journal of Biological Macromolecules (Elsevier), Associate Editor of PLOS Neglected Tropical Diseases, and a member of the editorial boards of several renowned international journals.

Prof. Tripathi is deeply committed to teaching and mentoring, encouraging curiosity and innovation in his students. He advocates for interdisciplinary science and actively supports the National Education Policy (NEP) 2020 by integrating research with academics and encouraging collaboration. His vision is to improve the academic environment and unify research efforts across Indian universities.